Raise Your Vibration, Transform Your Life

A Practical Guide for Attaining Better Health, Vitality and Inner Peace

Dawn James

Library and Archives Canada Cataloguing in Publication

James, Dawn, 1965-
    Raise your vibration, transform your life: a practical guide for attaining better health, vitality and inner peace / Dawn James.

ISBN 978-0-9865378-1-3

    1. Vibration. 2. Self-realization. I. Title.

BF637.S4J353 2010   131   C2010-900744-1

    Lotus Moon Press
    P.O. Box 713 Uxbridge, ON Canada L9P 1N1
    Substantial discounts on bulk quantities of Lotus Moon Press publications are available to corporations, professional associations and other qualified organizations. For details, please contact Lotus Moon Press at the above address or send an email to lotusmoonpress@ymail.com.

Note to the reader: This book is not intended to dispense medical advice or prescribe the use of any technique as a form of treatment for physical, emotional or medical problems without the advice of a physician. The products and information contained in this book are not intended to diagnose, treat, cure or prevent any diseases or medical problems. The information is provided for educational purposes only. In the event you use any of the information in this book for yourself, which is your constitutional right, the author and publisher assume no responsibility for your actions.

Printed in Canada

Dedication

I dedicate this book to a woman whom I have never met in person. We have never spoken on the phone, or exchanged written or electronic communication, and yet she was able to give me a message—it was in a way a "key" to a door that needed to be opened. Metaphorically speaking, she placed the key in my hand and literally pointed to what I needed to open at this time. As a result, the subject of vibrational frequency has been at the forefront of my research, studies and experiences and has now manifested into this book to share with the rest of the world.

I dedicate *Raise Your Vibration, Transform Your Life: A Practical Guide for Attaining Better Health, Vitality and Inner Peace* to Sylvia Browne, spiritual teacher, psychic and a known Atlantean soul. How was she able to reach me without a letter, phone call, email, text, blog or the like? The answer to that question begins some 40 years ago when I was a young child. The term I use to describe this phenomenon is *dream share*. When I was a child, my mother I and would often share dreams. In other words, she would wake up and start telling me about a dream she had the night before. And as her story began to unfold, I would interrupt her and say *did you see the so and so*, and she would reply *yes*. *And was there a person wearing such and such*, and she would reply *yes*. Then she would continue telling me her dream. Apart from my mother, the only other person I have experienced dream share with is Sylvia Browne.

During the spring of 2005, I dreamt I was hosting a slumber party, and at this event was Sylvia Browne. She was chatting about this and that, and then I mentioned to her that there had been an energetic disturbance in my home and I noticed it was affecting my son. Over the past several months, his disposition had changed; he had become withdrawn and not as playful as he used to be. His grades in school were falling as well. Sylvia then stood up and told me to follow her. She walked into my son's room and pointed to what was causing the disturbance. She then gave me a very profound message. Needless to say, the following morning when I woke up, I walked into my son's room and removed the object. A few days later I noticed he was smiling more, his energy level was higher and within three short months there was noticeable improvement in his school grades.

Her message to me ignited my quest to learn more about vibrational frequency and how it can be used to enhance health and well-being, and how to prevent lower vibrational frequencies that have adverse effects on our emotional, physical and mental well-being.

Sylvia, this book represents the first of several doors that your "key" has helped me unlock. There are two more doors on the horizon for me to open. I feel blessed for being open to receive your message, and I am eternally grateful for having the opportunity to share this subject with the world. Perhaps one day I will have the good fortune to meet you in person.

Being Conscious

We are what we eat

We are what we drink

We are what we say

We are what we think.

With that in mind, I say to mankind:

Conscious eating

Conscious drinking

Conscious speaking and

Conscious thinking.

Conscious Being!

~ Dawn James

Contents

Preface	vii
Acknowledgments	xi
The Vibration and Health Connection	1
Thoughts	5
Words	9
Making Conscious Choices	13
The Vibration of Food and Drink	19
Detoxification	51
Vibration and Mass Media	67
Brain Waves-Stress-Health Connection	71
Breath Work	79
Essential Oils	87
The Chakra-Vibration-Health Connection	91
Vibration Work with Essential Oils	95
Vibration Work with Gems and Crystals	99
Vibration Work with Sound and Color	103
Spend Time in Nature	113
Spend Time in Silence and Meditation	119
Associate with Positive People	125
Attitude of Gratitude	129
The Vibration of Forgiveness	133
Living in Joy	137
Living in Love	145
Your Notes	149
Your Personal Action Plan	150
Glossary	151
References	155
About the Author	158

Preface

This book is a compilation of over two decades of research, study, interviews, observations and direct experiences in the relationship between personal vibration frequency and health (mental, physical, emotional, psychological, spiritual), as well as the effects of higher vibrations on perception, attitude and consciousness.

Vibrational frequency is the constant rate of electrical flow that is measurable between two points. Quantum physics has shown that we are bioelectric beings with electric currents flowing through our cells, nerves and muscles. In fact, bioelectricity is one of the fundamental forms of energy in the human body. Bioelectric potentials (potential energy) are generated by a number of different biological processes, and are used by our cells to govern metabolism and impulses within the central nervous system and brain function, and to regulate muscle contraction, to name a few. There are three types of electrical signals in human beings: The first signal originates in the brain, the second signal originates in the heart and the third signal, of unknown origin, is referred to as the *surface electrical potential*. Furthermore, the mind-body-spirit network is interdependent of and influenced by our personal vibratory rate and by changes in our vibrational frequency. When our vibrational frequency is suppressed due to stresses, toxins and external factors, the body weakens, the mind becomes dull or agitated and our connection to spirit/higher consciousness/Divine Wisdom is interrupted or short-circuited. Ancient teachings, as well as modern medicine, have shown that we all have the ability to increase the rate of electric flow within our body and energy systems, and that there is a direct correlation between raising our vibratory rate and our ability to repel disease, increase vitality and raise consciousness. This practical guide offers a multitude of simple and effective ways to raise your personal vibratory rate—while providing insights on the connectivity between thoughts, attitudes, behaviors, stress and health.

Why raise your personal vibration? By learning how to strengthen your mind-body-spirit network, your mind will become tranquil, your physical body will become stronger and healthier and your energy systems will become more fluid and balanced. By applying the methods and exercises presented in this book, you will become unmovable and untouchable psychologically by lower vibrations, including emotions such as fear or pain, as well as by unpleasant people and situations. The assimilation of these changes will allow a greater flow of life force energy into your mind and body, thereby raising your vibrational frequency for improved health, and raising your perception so that life becomes more enjoyable. In addition, you will begin to encounter other people with higher vibrations, and attract positive and pleasant situations into your life.

You are truly an energetic being designed to vibrate at a high frequency. You were designed to learn and to create.

You were also designed to have the ability to accept the responsibility to be accountable for your own self-improvement. You are capable of manifesting the best of yourself when you consciously take action, and cease reacting to emotions and other people and events in your life.

My intention is for this book to provide you with insights and practical steps to take to raise your personal vibration for improved health and increased vitality, and to cultivate inner peace. Your success can be measured by the strength of your willpower and self-discipline to practice the exercises and apply high vibrational frequencies and vibrational mechanics to benefit your physical, electrical, biological, chemical, emotional, psychological and spiritual self.

Acknowledgments

I thank my husband, Ian, for his continuous support, encouragement and love as I progress on my spiritual journey. Special thanks to my father, Hollis, for being my first spiritual teacher and introducing me to the world of holistic living and healing practices from cultures around the globe. He also instilled in me the importance of "connecting to source" and inner wisdom. My deepest gratitude also to my countless teachers, of both the physical and the spiritual worlds, whom I have learned from and been inspired by, and who have guided me to this moment.

This book would not have been possible without the guiding help of some living angels who walk among us: namely, my editor, Andrea Lemieux; James Dewar and Sue Reynolds from The Writers' Circle of Durham Region, Ontario; and Sylvia Browne for entering my dreams and handing me "the key." Thank you, all!

Dawn

The Vibration and Health Connection

Everything in nature vibrates at specific frequencies, including our very cells. Scientists are rediscovering that certain frequencies can prevent disease, and certain frequencies can destroy disease. This is the fundamental basis of the connection between vibrational frequency and the state of our health.

Furthermore, scientific research has shown that different parts of our body have their own sonic signature. In other words, the sound of the cells in a healthy heart is different from the sound of the cells in an unhealthy heart. When parts of the body become diseased, they no longer vibrate at their prime resonant frequency; in other words, they no longer produce the correct sound waves. If we can correct the body's sonic signature—that is, change the vibration—then we can restore the body to a healthy state.

Stresses in various forms (such as emotional, physical and environmental) contribute to poor health, unbalanced energy systems, suppression of the immune system and suppression of vibration levels.

To counteract various stresses and reestablish the prime resonant frequency of our cells, organs and physical body as a whole, we need to apply the laws of vibrational mechanics. The first law states that *a lower vibrational frequency must yield to a higher vibrational frequency.* For example, when our energy flow is impeded by stress or toxins, our vibrational frequency begins to decrease, and this causes us to lose energy by reducing our ability to access universal life force, or *prana.* As our energy becomes stagnant, our health declines. Prolonged states of low vibrational frequency cause our cells to mutate and organs to degenerate, ultimately resulting in disease. By applying a higher vibrational frequency to a lower vibration, the lower vibration naturally tries to resonate at a higher frequency—and it is in the process of resonation that energy flow is restored, stresses are released and health improves.

The second law of vibration states that *the identity structure and energy pattern of an object are affected by changes in vibrational frequency.* If we take a pot of water, for example, and place it on a heated stove, the identity structure of the water molecules will change from water to steam and eventually moisture/humidity as the vibrational frequency increases with higher temperatures. Another example of the second law of vibration is depicted in Dr. Emoto's book *The Miracle of Water*,[1] where we can see how words that are spoken or written on labels affixed to a glass of water have an effect on the structure of the water molecules as the water begins to freeze. When positive words are used, the water molecules form beautiful symmetrical hexagonal patterns; however, when negative words are used, the water molecules that form are asymmetrical, incongruent—they make no recognizable geometric form—and sometimes look like lopsided balloons. The same effect holds true for our body, which is composed of 70 to 75% water. Our cell structure is directly impacted—positively or negatively—by changes in vibrational frequency.

As energetic sentient beings, our emotions are also encoded in our cell formation through bioelectric impulses we experience every minute of the day. Our cells respond to our emotions by generating a quality of energy that reflects those emotions. If emotions are positive, then the energy created will be light, refined and ethereal in nature. Similarly, if emotions are negative, then the energy created will be heavy, sluggish, constricted. Our emotional health is therefore vital to our physical health. This brings us to the third law of vibration.

I am certain you have heard the old adage "what goes around, comes around." Well, this captures the essence of the third and final vibrational law: *Changes in mental attitude and thoughts can affect the vibrational frequency of yourself, others you interact with and your experiences.* For instance, if my mental attitude is negative, despondent or depressed, and I see the world from a place of lack or from the belief that I am a victim of circumstances, then my entire being will vibrate in a perfect state to receive dull, heavy, depressing vibrations from myself and others (i.e., like attracts like). However, if my mental attitude is positive, alert and optimistic, then my entire being will vibrate in a perfect state to receive light, uplifting and higher vibrations. An energy field that vibrates at a high level of frequency draws positive, healthy, happy experiences, whereas an energy that is low in vibration draws experiences that we consider negative or unhealthy. Herein lies the direct correlation between raising your personal vibration, improving health, increasing vitality and experiencing inner peace.

Thoughts

Your body is physiologically tied to your thoughts, beliefs and attitudes. To be healthy, you have to recognize the connection that exists between your mind, body and spirit. Positive thinking is a first step in raising your personal vibration. Scientific studies, and now scientific instruments, are being used to measure the effect of positive and negative thinking with respect to disease. Negative thoughts have just as much power as positive ones. They slowly chip away at you, resulting in poor self-esteem, depression and even illness. How can one person succumb to a particular circumstance, while another person can thrive in the same situation? It simply boils down to mental attitude!

When you choose a thought, your brain cells are affected. These cells vibrate and send off electromagnetic waves. The more you concentrate on those thoughts, the greater the amplitude of vibration of those cells, and the electric waves, in turn, become stronger.

Positive thinking can raise your vibration up to 10 hertz (Hz), whereas negative thinking can lower your vibration by as much as 15 Hz. These measurements come from Bruce Tainio of Tainio Technology in Cheney, Washington. His company developed new equipment to measure the biofrequency of humans and foods. The number one way to start feeling better is to start thinking positively. Strive to maintain the positive attitude that you will be triumphant in the end, no matter what the circumstances.

To do this, first begin by observing your thoughts. Detach from them and pay attention when a negative thought enters your consciousness. When this happens, immediately replace it with a positive thought. For example, if you are driving on the highway and traffic is moving slowly and you find you are dwelling on thoughts such as "I am going to be late"—the negative thought of a hopeless victim—instead, replace that thought with, "I will arrive exactly when I am supposed to arrive," which is a positive thought that reflects your inner knowing and confident self.

There is a saying: "You get what you expect." In other words, if you think you are going to fail at something, most likely you will fail. Why? Because your energy follows your thoughts and you begin to create or manifest what you believe and expect.

Remember that it is *you* who is originating those electric waves and also determining the density of them by your own free will. And know that it is you who has put your whole being in that particular vibration.

Personal Story: Changing Expectations

A few years ago, I decided that I needed to improve my cardiovascular health, having had a desk job for over 20 years and being overly dependent on a car to get me from place to place. So our family trekked to the nearest high school with a 400-meter running track. My husband, a former track-and-field buff, said, "Let's do it. Let's run a lap!" My first thought was, "400 meters? There is no way I can jog 400 meters non-stop." Truth be told, in my first two attempts I jogged less than 200 meters. Then, out of the mouth of my 10-year-old daughter came, "Just put one foot in front of the other, don't worry about the distance, just your two feet moving." Ahhh. That sounds simple enough. I held the thought, "I can move my feet," and I starting jogging. I counted "one" for my left foot and "two" for my right foot: one, two, one, two, silently and steadily—and to my surprise, I managed to jog around the entire track. By removing the negative thought that I could not run 400 meters and focusing on the thought, "I can move my feet," I was in fact able to jog the full distance.

Replace a negative expectation with a positive expectation and see what happens! You will be pleasantly surprised.

Positive imagery can also influence actual outcomes. Using the mind, you can make thought reality; for example, you can visualize the progress toward health, and thereby restore health. For instance, if you feel a migraine coming on, visualize the energy that is building up in your head, then picture an opening in the crown of your head where you allow that excess energy to be gently released and float away like a cloud. Then visualize your energy as a column of light that begins at the top of your head and ends at the soles of your feet. Your column is strong, with the same width from top to bottom—completely balanced energy. The most important element of visualization is that you have hope and faith that a way is going to open up for you—after all, nothing lasts forever, not even the present circumstance you may be facing. Positive imagery immediately relieves stress, increases confidence and channels your energy in a positive direction to manifest desired results.

Words

Positive speech, affirmations and prayers can improve your health and emotional well-being. When you affirm your beliefs with your speech, your words create a positive vibration that can reshape your mind and body.

Affirmations are simple statements that create health and abundance for you. When you speak and think positively, you create positive circumstances.

Here are some guidelines for affirmations:

- Use positive action words such as "I am," "I choose," "I deserve."
- Decide what areas of your life you want to improve, then create a list of positive affirmations you can say *daily*.
- Firmly believe in what you are saying.

Here are some examples of positive affirmations you can use to improve your health and well-being:

- Healing happens each time I rest, relax and enjoy myself.
- I deserve to be disease free.
- I heal any condition that affects me, knowing my body seeks balance and regeneration.
- I am energetic and filled with energy.

- I am able to sleep peacefully and wake feeling rested.
- I have the willpower to defeat disease and illness.
- I love and honor my body.
- I accept the power of my being to produce health, love and joy in my life.
- I treat myself respectfully.
- I choose health, healing and happiness.

Watch your words! In the principles of *Ma'at*—the ancient Egyptian concept of truth, balance, morality and justice—there is a document known as the "42 Negative Confessions."[2] It is also called the "Affirmations of Innocence," because the person uttering the statements is affirming what moral principles they have not transgressed. These affirmations can be classified into three categories: Right Thought, Right Speech and Right Action. Here are a few affirmations regarding Right Speech:

- I have not uttered lies.
- I have not uttered curses.
- I have not slandered [anyone].
- I have not blasphemed.
- I have not been a stirrer up of strife.
- I have never raised my voice.
- I have not pried into matters.
- I have not multiplied my words in speaking.

Vibration Exercise: Non-negative Speech

Try not to say anything negative for a period of two hours per day for the next seven days, and then gradually extend this to four hours, then eight hours a day. You will be amazed at how often you have an urge make a negative comment. If you can witness the thought, if it arises and you recognize it as negative, you can simply not allow negative words to occur. The more you witness your negativity, the less you will be negative! By doing this exercise, you will also realize that you cannot improve a situation by injecting negativity into it. The energy you expended on being negative will now be used for making quiet observations and increasing feelings of serenity, acceptance and peace.

It may seem difficult to break a negative habit such as gossiping, but the next time you get the urge to gossip, try to remember this definition and decide if you really want to participate: *Gossip is the transference of emotional poison from one person to another*. Try not to spend time listening or engaging in negative conversations or gossip, being boastful (ego-mind), arguing, yelling or telling lies. These forms of communication are damaging and can drag your personal vibration to low levels quickly.

The following figure illustrates how positive beliefs, then thinking, visualization, feeling, speaking and action all progressively raise your vibration and lead to good health.

Good Health

↑

Positive Action

↑

Positive Speaking

↑

Positive Feeling

↑

Positive Visualization

↑

Positive Thinking

↑

Positive Beliefs

Making Conscious Choices

We are creators and we live to create. Every choice that we make creates consequences—for others as well as for ourselves.

Are you consciously aware of what you are creating, and do you fully accept the consequences of your choices? Life is always presenting us with different courses of action to take. If you find a course of action that produces consequences that you *are not* willing to assume responsibility for, then don't choose it! And if you find a course of action that produces consequences that you *are* willing to assume responsibility for, then move in that direction. The latter is about making responsible conscious choices.

There are three aspects of our being that influence our attitudes, beliefs, thoughts and, eventually, our actions: *Free Will, Ego* and *Divine Inner Wisdom.*

Free Will

Thanks to free will, you always have an opportunity to choose. The question is, will you choose consciously or unconsciously? The main difference between making conscious and unconscious choices is knowing what you are feeling. If you don't know what you are feeling, you will create unconsciously. If you live your life with actions and thoughts in autopilot and you are unconscious of aspects of yourself, such as being angry or jealous, hurt or bored, then you are living outside your field of awareness, and these aspects of yourself have power over you; you are giving them permission to do as they please.

Ego

Thanks to ego, there exists a concept of separateness, or duality, which manifests the belief that one must have control over others, leading to exploitation or slavery; control over resources, where we find mass production for economic benefit; and control over other countries, which can lead to wars and further exploitation and mass production for economic benefit. Conversely, if ego did not exist, then the concept of unity would thrive; in other words, if we are all one and part of the same whole, or source, then I would not need to take from you or exploit you, because I would ultimately be taking from myself and exploiting myself. It is this concept of separateness that creates feelings of fear, pain, jealousy, greed, judgment, blame, inferiority and superiority. Ego will also choose to satisfy its desires and needs for external power, regardless of the consequences to others or itself.

Divine Inner Wisdom

Thanks to Divine Inner Wisdom, you have the opportunity to be aware of and observe, learn and appreciate all aspects of your being. And in being fully conscious of yourself, you are able to choose the best response to all circumstances you encounter.

Gary Zukav, author of *The Seat of the Soul*, in an interview with Dr. Jeffrey Mishlove, eloquently describes this as authentic power:[3]

> We choose to align ourselves with our souls, to strive toward authentic power ... by choosing how we are going to respond, moment by moment, to the experience that we find ourselves in in our lives. And if you look at your life as your learning environment, offering you, at each moment, maximal, optimal, optimal opportunities to learn, give yourself permission at each moment to choose the most positive behavior. This is how you align your personality with your soul. This is how you acquire authentic power.

And this is how you make conscious choices—by allowing your Divine Inner Wisdom to guide you every moment of every day.

We all possess certain habits we would like to break or "addictions" we would like to overcome, such as smoking, shopping, eating the wrong foods and procrastination. To overcome these habits or addictions, we need to have willpower and self-discipline. They are vital to manifesting inner strength, self-mastery and decisiveness.

Willpower is the ability to overcome negative traits or habits. It is the ability to control or reject unnecessary or harmful impulses. It is the ability to arrive at a decision and follow it with perseverance until its successful completion. It is the inner power that overcomes the desire to indulge in unnecessary and destructive habits, and the inner strength that overcomes inner emotional and mental resistance for taking action.

Self-discipline is the companion of willpower. It provides the stamina to persevere in whatever one does. It offers the ability to withstand hardships and difficulties, whether physical, emotional or mental. It grants the ability to reject immediate satisfaction in order to gain something better, but which requires effort and time.

By developing these two traits, you will increase your awareness of the inner, subconscious impulses, and gain the ability to reject them when they are not for your higher good.

Willpower and self-discipline help us to choose our behavior and reactions, instead of being ruled by them.

You need both of them in order to make truly conscious choices. The stronger they are, the more control you have over your thoughts, your interactions with others and, ultimately, your experiences. (Remember vibration law number three from the chapter "The Vibration and Health Connection"!)

When you are the master of your mind, you can enjoy inner peace and happiness. External forces, events, circumstances will not sway you nor overpower your peace of mind.

These abilities are essential for self-growth and spiritual growth.

Personal Story: From Making Unconscious to Conscious Choices

I had a client who would often eat whenever she became bored. To pass the time, she would stroll into the kitchen pantry and eat whatever she fancied. Weeks later, she would complain about the weight she was gaining. We began by exploring her feelings of boredom. After an in-depth conversation, she realized that she was not, in fact, bored, but was really feeling lonely. She lived alone and had no pets or any family members living in her town. She wanted to be more physically active, but she wanted someone to do it with and to spend time with. We discussed the possibility of her joining a local fitness class where she could meet new people, get some exercise, have more fun and, hopefully, make new friends. Which she did in no time. By getting in touch with her *real* feelings, she was able to shed her unconscious emotional eating habits and choose a positive way of resolving her feelings of loneliness. She was now making conscious choices.

By exploring your feelings, you can uncover aspects of yourself and increase awareness of behaviors, attitudes and beliefs that are no longer beneficial to you. By increasing self-awareness, you are able to choose an alternate course of action and adopt new behaviors and attitudes and beliefs that are more beneficial, positive and harmonious to you. You are now living consciously and making conscious decisions for your greater good.

The Vibration of Food and Drink

I am sure you have heard the old adage, "You are what you eat." One of the food challenges we face today is that many of the foods we eat contain ingredients and are processed in a manner that our organs and cells were *not* designed to digest! As a result of eating denatured and processed foods, coupled with toxins from high-volume food manufacturing, we are polluting our body and suppressing our vibrational frequency.

Most nutritionists classify foods into three categories: carbohydrates, proteins and fats. Although most of us receive information about selecting foods from the various food groups, we do not receive adequate information on the optimal form in which foods should be consumed to ensure good health and nutrition. The form in which we consume our foods directly correlates to the level of vibration of the foods, and whether the foods provide the required nutrients to our cells.

When our cells do not obtain sufficient nutrients from the foods we eat, they begin to starve and seek out and cling to fat and store it away. Why fat? Because fat has twice the caloric power of carbohydrates or proteins.

The table below illustrates the vibration levels of canned and processed foods and certain unprocessed foods.

Vibration Levels of Food Groups

Food	Vibration Levels in Hertz (Hz)
Canned foods	0 Hz
Processed foods*	0 Hz
Fresh produce	Up to 15 Hz
Fresh herbs	12–27 Hz
Dry herbs	2–27 Hz

*The Center for Food Safety states that it has been estimated that more than 70% of all processed foods contain genetically engineered ingredients.[4]

Fact: In 2008, the Austrian government released research results confirming that GM crops threaten human fertility in both genders. As a result, Austria banned all biotech foods.[5]

Why do canned foods have a vibration level of 0 Hz? It is because canning preserves food by heating it in airtight, vacuum-sealed containers; this process removes oxygen, destroys enzymes and kills most microorganisms that may be present in the food. The canning process also compromises the quantity and quality of water-soluble vitamins contained in the food.

Why do processed foods have a vibration level of 0 Hz? It is because processed food is denatured, is usually modified in structure and composition and contains additives, the majority of which are unnatural and provide no nutrients to human cells. Many of the food additives are designed to trick our senses by making food look, smell and taste better, while "appearing" to be whole and fresh. However, these additives cannot trick our digestive system!

So what can you consume to raise your vibration? If you want to raise your vibration through the consumption of food, then you need to eat foods in their most natural and organic state, with the highest amount of life force energy, the least amount of pesticides and the least amount of processing to ensure your cells receive the nutrients they need so your organs can function optimally.

1. Essential Fatty Acids

There are 100 trillion cells in your body that require essential fatty acids (EFAs) in order to function properly. EFAs are fat in a raw form, whereby the molecules and electrons are in their natural state. The key word here is *natural*! EFAs have the following health benefits:

- Reduce the risk of cardiovascular disease.
- Improve brain function, including mood, behavior, vision and intelligence.
- Reduce depression.
- Increase energy.
- Improve glandular and organ function.
- Bring about faster recovery for healing.
- Contribute to better skin, hair and nails.
- Improve digestion.

Scientists classify essential fatty acids into two types: omega-3 fatty acids and omega-6 fatty acids, depending on their chemical composition. Technically, the omega-3 fatty acids are alpha-linolenic acid, stearidonic acid and two others called EPA and DHA. Alpha-linolenic acid is found mainly in flaxseed oil, canola oil, soybeans, walnuts, hemp seeds and dark green leafy vegetables. Stearidonic acid is found in rarer types of seeds and nuts, including black currant seeds. EPA and DHA are present in cold-water fish, including salmon, trout, sardines, mackerel and cod. Cod liver oil is a popular nutritional supplement for omega-3 EFAs.

Omega-6 fatty acids are more common in the North American diet than the omega-3 EFAs. These include linoleic acid (LA), which is found in safflower, olive, almond, sunflower, hemp, soybean, walnut, pumpkin, sesame and flaxseed oils, and gamma-linolenic acid (GLA), which is found in some seeds and evening primrose oil.

The ratio of omega-6 to omega-3 in the North American diet today is 10:1 to 15:1, whereas experts recommend an ideal ratio of 1:1 to 3:1.

2. Proteins in Their Natural and Organic State

Proteins are made up of sequences of amino acids. There are 20 different amino acids. Our body is able to produce 12 of them. We have to get the remaining amino acids from the foods we eat.

The amino acids that our body is able to produce are called non-essential amino acids. The amino acids that our body is unable to produce, and must obtain from food, are called essential amino acids.

The essential amino acids are isoleucine, leucine, lysine, methionine, phenylalanine, threonine, tryptophan and valine. Non-essential amino acids are arginine, alanine, asparagine, aspartic acid, cysteine, glutamine, glutamic acid, glycine, proline, serine and tyrosine. Semi-essential amino acids are ones that can sometimes be made internally if conditions are right. Histidine is considered semi-essential because the body does not always require dietary sources of it.

Fact: Young barley grass leaves, from the seedlings of the barley plant, contain all nine essential amino acids.

The most common sources of protein are meat, poultry, fish and seafood, eggs, dairy products and grains and legumes (dried beans and peas).

Regarding meat protein, it is important to note that *excessive* consumption of meat depletes the body of calcium! Why? Because meat is very low in calcium and extremely high in phosphorus, which has adverse health effects, as described by Dr. Mary Ruth Swope in her book *The Green Leaves of Barley*:[6]

> [M]any research studies allude to the fact that high phosphorus and/or phosphoric acid (found in meats and soft drinks) pulls calcium out of bony structures (bones, teeth and nails) in the process of digestion and assimilation. This has a disastrous effect on bone density, leaving them porous and spongy. When calcium is pulled out of the bones, it is released through the kidneys, resulting in stone formation (kidney stones) before it is excreted.

Furthermore, animal proteins contain sharp needle-like substances called spicules and a type of fat called kilo microns, which your body *cannot* digest. When animal proteins are cooked, their molecular structure is altered from an absorbable state to a non-absorbable state. This unabsorbed, heat-altered animal protein will putrefy in your intestine.

Key Message:
Limit the amount of meat protein you eat and refer to section 7 below, "Digestive Enzymes," and the chapter "Detoxification" for additional recommendations.

3. Simple and Manufactured Sugars versus Complex Sugars

Not all sugars are created equally! Sugars are classified as either simple or complex. Simple sugars have one to three units of sugar linked together in single molecules. Complex sugars, also known as complex carbohydrates, or starches, are made up of long, complicated strings of sugar molecules linked together. In general, simple sugars are refined, processed, have little nutritional value and enter the bloodstream very quickly. Complex sugars, on the other hand, are the least refined and can contain vitamins, minerals and nutrients, and they take longer for the body to break down.

There are two main classes of complex sugars (carbohydrates):

i. **Starchy carbohydrates**, which include foods such as brown rice, white and sweet potatoes, oatmeal and whole-grain pastas and grains.

ii. **Fibrous carbohydrates**, which include foods such as asparagus, broccoli, cauliflower, onions, mushrooms, spinach and peppers, and can also be found in most varieties of dark green leafy vegetables.

"Manufactured" sugar, a group of related compounds, termed *sugars* by chemists, consists of corn sugar (glucose or dextrose), fruit sugar (fructose or levulose), milk sugar (lactose) and malt sugar (maltose). These manufactured sugars, as well as simple sugars, may provide a quick source of energy, but they also cause a rapid increase in blood sugar levels. Consuming large quantities of foods that contain these sugars have been linked to adverse health affects, such as obesity, tooth decay, gout, diabetes, insulin resistance and heart disease.

> **Grocery Shopping Tip:**
> Try to avoid carbohydrates that include the following words in their ingredients: **bleached, enriched, processed** or **refined**. These processed and altered foods are often void of critical nutrient value and will do very little to fuel and energize your body.

Key Message #1:
Excess simple sugars = excess
calories with virtually *no* nutrient
value, and long-term adverse health
effects.

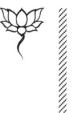

Key Message #2:
Complex sugars/carbohydrates often
contain vitamins, minerals and
nutrients that nourish the body.

Choose wisely!

4. Water

Water hydrates your body, helps oxygenate your cells and helps remove toxic impurities from your system. Therefore, it is important to consume water. But like food, the quality of the water you consume correlates directly with your ability to raise your vibration. Not all water is processed in the same manner. Unless you obtain your drinking water from a well or natural spring, most of the water you consume is processed either through water treatment plants or by corporations that bottle water for resale. There are many water brands on the market to choose from. Some water brands contain total dissolved solids (TDS) that survive standard filtration. Although you may not see them with the human eye, these totally dissolved solids, or sediment, are *not* absorbed by your body. They accumulate in your liver and add undue stress as your liver tries to filter them out. It is estimated that some 60,000 known possible chemicals can appear as TDS in bottled water. The use of distilled water was a means to avoid TDS; however, in recent years natural health professionals have warned that the process of distillation and, more recently, reverse osmosis (RO), are unnatural processes, kill vital nutrients and filter out minerals, leaving only H_2O.

Distilled water and RO-filtered water contain no minerals, simulating close to pure water. This pure water should be neutral with a pH value of 7. However, it measures acid pH! This is because pure water sucks in carbon dioxide from the atmosphere, especially if it is stored in thin plastic bottles! Although it measures acid pH, there are no acid minerals in that water. For this reason, distilled water or RO-filtered water should be stored in glass bottles or special plastic bottles that can block carbon dioxide penetration. Furthermore, consuming this filtered water will actually cause vital alkaline minerals to leach out of your body, leading to severe mineral deficiency over a prolonged period of time.

In order to hydrate your body optimally, you need to drink water that is alkaline and mineral rich. Alkaline spring water is the optimal choice; however, if you cannot obtain spring water, then a second choice is to drink alkaline water.

Alkaline water acts as a buffer to the acidic conditions of the body. As previously mentioned, processed food, soft drinks and refined sugars, as well as meat and dairy products, are acidic, and they contribute significantly to the build up of acid salts in our body tissues. Physical and mental stresses can also increase acid deposits in the body. Over the years, these stored acid salts become a burden to our system and are a potential danger to health. Alkaline water helps to neutralize acids and remove toxins from the body. It also acts as a conductor of electrochemical activity from cell to cell. Researchers have found that alkalizing the bloodstream can help the following conditions: asthma, angina, migraine headaches, back pain, colitis pain, constipation, heartburn and hiatal hernia, depression, chronic fatigue syndrome, high cholesterol, morning sickness, overweight problems and heart problems needing bypass surgery.

If you have difficulty obtaining alkaline water, then consider using pH drops to alkalize your filtered water. Ideally, water should have a pH between 9 and 10. Also ensure that you drink a sufficient amount of water, as the body loses approximately two and a half quarts of water each day through normal bodily functions (not including exercise); try to drink two and a half to three quarts (10–12 cups) of water daily to maintain optimal hydration.

In his book *The Hidden Truth of Cancer*,[7] Dr. Keiichi Morishita explains that if the blood accumulates excess acidic wastes year after year, cells begin to die, thus creating a platform for cancer growth.

Dr. Otto Warburg, Nobel Prize recipient, 1931 and 1944, also advises that "if our internal environment was changed from an acidic oxygen-deprived environment to an alkaline environment full of oxygen, viruses, bacteria and fungus cannot live."[8]

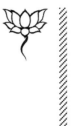 Key Message:
Water is a key element of life involved in many bodily functions, including hydration, oxygenation and detoxification; therefore, it is imperative that you consume the best quality water available to support a healthy internal environment.

5. Minerals

The minerals in our food depend on the minerals in the soil in which the food is grown or that the animals we eat consume. Our soils are supposed to contain seventeen minerals that are vital to human health and that are transferred to plants. However, aggressive modern farming techniques have contributed to the depletion of minerals in the soil.

The lack of minerals in our soil is evidenced by the need for constant fertilization. Plants need nitrogen, hydrogen, oxygen, chlorine, carbon, boron, sulfur, potassium, magnesium, phosphorus, iron, zinc, copper, manganese and molybdenum, some of which are commonly replaced through fertilizers to provide maximum crops through minimum investment. However, in addition to these minerals, humans need calcium, sodium, fluorine, bromine, chromium, iodine, silicon, selenium, beryllium, lithium, cobalt, vanadium and nickel, which would not necessarily be replaced through fertilization.[9] The difference between regular produce and "organic" produce is that organic produce is grown in soil that contains all 17 of the minerals vital to human health, without any pesticides! Regular produce is grown in soils lacking all 17 minerals, and often pesticides and chemical fertilizers are used. Organic produce may cost a premium over non-organic produce, but remember, you are what you eat! You can pay less up front for denatured, processed, genetically modified, nutrient-poor foods and end up paying for it later with poor health. The choice is always yours.

Some Organic Facts:

- "One teaspoon of compost-rich organic soil hosts 600 million to 1 billion helpful bacteria from 15,000 species. One teaspoon of chemically treated soil can host as few as 100 bacteria."[10]

- "It takes approximately 3,000 years for nature to produce 6 inches of topsoil. Every 28 years, 1 inch of topsoil is lost as a result of current farming practices. Organic bio-intensive farming can produce 6 inches of topsoil in as little as 50 years—60 times faster than the rate in nature."[10]

- Organic produce contains up to 10 times the mineral content of regular produce.

- Organic agriculture builds the health of the soil, providing the foundation for healthy crops and a livelihood for good stewards of the land.

- National organic standards require producers to use organic agricultural methods and materials that cover soil fertility, the application of manure, crop rotation and composting. National organic standards prohibit the use of municipal solid waste and sewage sludge as compost ingredients.

Food Sources of Minerals

Mineral	What It Does	Significant Food Sources
Sodium	Maintains fluid and electrolyte balance, supports muscle contraction and nerve impulse transmissions	salt, soy sauce, bread, milk, meats
Chloride	Maintains fluid and electrolyte balance, aids in digestion	salt, soy sauce, milk, eggs, meats
Potassium	Maintains fluid and electrolyte balance, cell integrity, muscle contractions and nerve impulse transmission	potatoes, acorn squash, artichoke, spinach, broccoli, carrots, green beans, tomato juice, avocado, grapefruit juice, watermelon, bananas, strawberries, cod, milk
Calcium	Formation of bones and teeth, supports blood clotting	milk, yogurt, Cheddar cheese, Swiss cheese, tofu, sardines, green beans, spinach, broccoli
Phosphorus	Formation of cells, bones and teeth; maintains acid-base balance	all animal foods (meats, fish, poultry, eggs, milk)

Food Sources of Minerals

Mineral	What It Does	Significant Food Sources
Iron	Part of the protein hemoglobin (carries oxygen throughout body's cells)	artichoke, parsley, spinach, broccoli, green beans, tomato juice, tofu, clams, shrimp, beef liver
Zinc	A part of many enzymes, involved in the production of genetic material and proteins, the transport of vitamin A, taste perception, wound healing, sperm production and the normal development of the fetus	spinach, broccoli, green peas, green beans, tomato juice, lentils, oysters, shrimp, crab, turkey (dark meat), lean ham, lean ground beef, lean sirloin steak, plain yogurt, Swiss cheese, tofu, ricotta cheese
Selenium	Antioxidant, works with vitamin E to protect the body from oxidation	seafood, meats, grains
Iodine	Component of thyroid hormones that help regulate growth, development and metabolic rate	salt, seafood, bread, milk, cheese

Food Sources of Minerals

Mineral	What It Does	Significant Food Sources
Copper	Necessary for the absorption and utilization of iron, supports the formation of hemoglobin and several enzymes	meats, liver, shellfish, nuts, legumes, whole grains, raisins, cherries, prunes
Manganese	Facilitates many cell processes	widespread in foods
Fluoride	Involved in the formation of bones and teeth, helps to make teeth resistant to decay	fluoridated drinking water, tea, seafood
Chromium	Associated with insulin and is required for the release of energy from glucose	vegetable oils, liver, brewer's yeast, whole grains, cheese, nuts
Molybdenum	Facilitates many cell processes	legumes, organ meats

Grains can be a rich source of minerals; however, the manner in which they are processed or prepared can affect their nutrient content.

There are two types of grain: enriched and whole. Enriched grain is grain that has been refined with some of the essential nutrients lost during processing added back. More often than not, however, synthetic vitamins are added back.

Whole grains contain health-promoting phytonutrients such as antioxidants, lignins and plant sterols, as well as fiber, which are lacking in enriched products. Whole grains include whole-grain bread, whole oats/oatmeal, whole-grain corn, brown and wild rice, whole rye, whole-grain barley, bulgur, triticale, buckwheat, millet, popcorn and quinoa.

Whole grains can also be sprouted, which can be a better way to consume them because sprouting breaks down the phytic acid in whole grains.[11] This is beneficial because phytic acid can prevent the absorption of minerals. Fermenting grain to make sourdough bread also helps make whole grains easier to digest.

Key Message #1:
A diet rich in unsprouted whole grains may lead to mineral deficiency and bone loss!

Key Message #2:
Sprouted whole grain does not promote mineral deficiency.

Key Message #3:
Organic produce contains more
minerals than non-organic produce,
as well as no pesticides.

6. Vitamins

Vitamins are classified as either water soluble or fat soluble. In humans there are 13 vitamins: four fat soluble (A, D, E and K) and nine water soluble (eight B vitamins and vitamin C). Water-soluble vitamins dissolve easily in water and, in general, are readily excreted from the body. Because they are not readily stored, consistent daily intake is important. Fat-soluble vitamins are absorbed through the intestinal tract with the help of lipids (fats). Because they are more likely to accumulate in the body, they are more likely to lead to hypervitaminosis than are water-soluble vitamins. In addition, excessive consumption of the fat-soluble vitamins may lead to vitamin overdose or vitamin poisoning.

In my opinion, the best-quality vitamins are derived from nutrient-rich, natural organic foods rather than from manufactured supplements that are added back to refined food.

Food Sources of Vitamins

Vitamin	What It Does	Significant Food Sources
B_1 (thiamin)	Supports energy metabolism and nerve function	spinach, green peas, watermelon, tomato juice, sunflower seeds, lean ham, lean pork chops, soy milk
B_2 (riboflavin)	Supports energy metabolism, normal vision and skin health	spinach, broccoli, mushrooms, eggs, milk, liver, oysters, clams
B_3 (niacin)	Supports energy metabolism, skin health, nervous system and digestive system	spinach, potatoes, tomato juice, lean ground beef, chicken breast, tuna (canned in water), liver, shrimp
Biotin	Supports energy metabolism, fat synthesis, amino acid metabolism, glycogen synthesis	widespread in foods
Pantothenic acid	Supports energy metabolism	widespread in foods
B_{12}	Used in new cell synthesis, helps break down fatty acids and amino acids, supports nerve cell maintenance	meats, poultry, fish, shellfish, milk, eggs

Food Sources of Vitamins

Vitamin	What It Does	Significant Food Sources
C (ascorbic acid)	Supports collagen synthesis, amino acid metabolism, helps iron absorption, immunity, antioxidant	spinach, broccoli, red bell peppers, snow peas, tomato juice, grapefruit juice, mango, orange, kiwi, strawberries
A (retinol)	Supports vision, skin, bone and tooth growth, immunity and reproduction	mango, broccoli, carrots, butternut squash, sweet potatoes, tomato juice, pumpkin, beef liver
D	Promotes bone mineralization	self-synthesis via sunlight, fortified milk, egg yolk, liver, fatty fish
E	Antioxidant, used for regulation of oxidation reactions, supports cell membrane stabilization	polyunsaturated plant oils (soybean, corn and canola oils), wheat germ, sunflower seeds, tofu, avocado, sweet potatoes, shrimp, cod
K	Supports synthesis of blood-clotting proteins, regulates blood calcium	Broccoli, Brussels sprouts, green leafy vegetables, spinach, cabbage, liver

7. Digestive Enzymes

Digestive enzymes, which are found in raw foods and produced by our body, break down food particles so they can be absorbed. The action of the enzymes in the digestive process starts in the mouth with the mechanical process of chewing. From the moment we think (or see or smell) a particular food, saliva is produced. Saliva lubricates the food and it contains the enzyme amylase (ptyalin), which helps break down starchy foods. When the food reaches the stomach, almost an hour passes before the body's own digestive enzymes are secreted. In the meantime, digestion relies on the enzymes present in the food, and if these food enzymes are lacking, an important step in the digestive process is lost.

Thanks to the convenience of precooked, processed, genetically modified and pasteurized foods, a vast majority of people consume enzymatically dead food! Naturally occurring enzymes found in foods are deactivated by heat above 118 degrees Fahrenheit. In other words, the high heat of cooking, processing and pasteurizing destroys vitamins and digestive enzymes in the food.

So what does this have to do with your health? By consuming foods devoid of enzymes, your body has to work extra hard (mainly through the pancreas) to produce enzymes to digest your food. Eventually, your body cannot produce enough enzymes for proper digestion, or enough metabolic enzymes for proper care of each organ, leading to the degeneration of your pancreas. Also, as we age, the body's ability to produce enzymes decreases.

The results of enzyme deficiency can include the following:

- Digestion is delayed during the essential 30 to 50 minutes after eating.
- Food is incompletely broken down, which allows undigested food to enter the colon, where bacteria can feed on it, causing such problems as toxicity, gas and bloating.
- Essential nutrients are not released and cannot be absorbed by the body, leading to nutritional deficiency.
- Digestive stress occurs and immune function is impaired.

How do you counteract this internal stress and regain some balance in the digestive process? By taking supplemental digestive enzymes when eating certain foods.

The main benefits of using digestive enzymes are that they replace the enzymes that were lost in the processing, cooking or pasteurization of foods, and they allow your naturally produced metabolic enzymes to do their job of running your organs and maintaining a proper weight.

Specific enzymes work on specific foods. You need the right type of enzyme for the food you want it to break down. Think of the foods you have problems with, and then choose a product that contains at least some of the enzymes needed for their digestion. The following chart lists the common enzymes and the foods they act on.

Enzymes and What They Do

Enzyme	What It Does
Amylase	Breaks down carbohydrates, starches and sugars, which are prevalent in potatoes, fruits, vegetables and many snack foods
Lactase	Breaks down lactose (milk sugar)
Diastase	Digests vegetable starch
Sucrase	Digests complex sugars and starches
Maltase	Breaks down disaccharides to monosaccharides (malt sugars)
Invertase	Breaks down sucrose (table sugar)
Glucoamylase	Breaks down starch to glucose
Alpha-galactosidase	Facilitates digestion of beans, legumes, seeds, roots, soy products
Protease	Breaks down proteins found in meats, nuts, eggs and cheese
Pepsin	Breaks down proteins into peptides
Peptidase	Breaks down small peptide proteins into amino acids
Trypsin	Derived from animal pancreas; breaks down proteins
Alpha-chymotrypsin	An animal-derived enzyme; breaks down proteins
Bromelain	Derived from pineapple; breaks down a broad spectrum of proteins, has anti-inflammatory properties, effective over very wide pH range

Enzymes and What They Do

Enzyme	What It Does
Papain	Derived from raw papaya; effective over broad range of substrates and pH, works well breaking down small and large proteins
Lipase	Breaks down fats found in most dairy products, nuts, oils and meat
Cellulase	Breaks down cellulose, plant fiber; enzymes produced chiefly by fungi, bacteria and protozoans

Tip: To combat enzyme deficiency try to increase the amount of raw food in your diet and include enzyme supplements with meals containing cooked or processed foods. A good digestive formula contains a variety of enzymes to address every food group and is not animal based. Animal-based enzymes have a much narrower pH range than vegetable-based enzymes. They are designed by nature to work in the specific range of acidity found in the animal source's system. Vegetable-based enzymes are effective in a broader pH range, which makes them more effective for a longer period in both the stomach and the intestines. A broad-based enzyme supplement not only enables digestion, but also reduces stress on the pancreas by reducing its need to produce enzymes, and the immune system by freeing enzymes for other purposes. Supplements should be taken during a meal, or within a half hour before or after a meal, and they can be taken in capsule form or sprinkled into water.[12]

Key Message:
Destress the internal digestive
system by increasing the consump-
tion of natural, organic, nutrient-
rich, enzyme-rich foods. This will
support optimal organ, cell and
blood function and allow energies
to flow with ease, facilitating the
raising of your personal vibration
frequency.

The Fatal-Four Beverages

I recall my grandmother saying "too much of one thing ain't good for nothing." That would apply to what I call the *fatal-four beverages*.

1. Alcohol

Excessive alcohol intake can harm the body's immune system in two ways:

a. It produces an overall nutritional deficiency, depriving the body of valuable immune-boosting nutrients.

b. Alcohol consumed in excess can reduce the ability of white blood cells to kill germs. Large amounts of alcohol suppress the ability of the white blood cells to multiply and inhibit the action of killer white cells on cancer cells. Damage to the immune system increases in proportion to the quantity of alcohol consumed.

2. Coffee

Excess coffee has been known to influence, contribute to and/or cause the following:

a. Emotional and physical stress: Caffeine stimulates the excretion of stress hormones, which can increase anxiety, irritability, muscle tension and insomnia, and decrease immune function.

b. Heart disease: Both decaf and regular coffee increase cholesterol and homocysteine, the biochemical that science has linked to increased risk of heart disease.

c. Hypoglycemia: Caffeine causes a release of glycogen by the liver, which can generate wild swings in blood sugar, causing attacks of hypoglycemia (low blood sugar). Hypoglycemia has a variety of unpleasant symptoms, including weakness, nervousness, sweating and heart palpitations.

d. Increased cholesterol: Certain molecules found in coffee beans are known to raise levels of low-density lipoproteins (LDLs) in humans—which result in higher total cholesterol levels.

e. Osteoporosis: According to osteoporosis expert Robert Heaney of Creighton University in Omaha, you lose up to 5 milligrams of calcium for every six ounces of regular coffee (or two cans of soda) you drink. As little as 300 to 400 mg of caffeine a day doubles the risk of hip fracture.[13]

Possible addiction: People who quit coffee often experience withdrawal symptoms such as fatigue, headache, decreased energy, difficulty concentrating and even depression.

f. Risks during pregnancy: Heavy consumption of coffee during pregnancy increases the risk of still-births and low-birth-weight infants. New mothers and infants are also at risk of iron deficiency anemia, as coffee also interferes with the absorption of supplemental iron.

g. Weight gain: Caffeine increases the risk of long-term weight gain by increasing stress hormones and creating a greater risk of hypoglycemia (low blood sugar), which stimulates appetite.

3. Soda

Do you drink regular or "diet" sodas or soft drinks? There are countless types of sodas on the market. Here are a few of the many things that make sodas harmful to your health:

a. All sodas contain excess phosphorus. Although phosphorus is a necessary component for bone formation, excess phosphorus blocks calcium absorption. When your body cannot obtain calcium from your blood, it will draw calcium from your bones, affecting jaws, teeth, hips and spine.

b. All sodas contain carbonic acid, which increases the acidity of the blood, causing pH levels to be out of balance. (Please see the chapter "Detoxification" below for more information on pH levels.)

c. Most sodas contain caffeine. The dangers of excess caffeine were noted above. In addition, excess caffeine consumption increases the urinary excretion of calcium.

d. Most sodas contain sugar or sugar substitutes, especially aspartame. The problem with consuming refined sugar was noted above under "Simple and Manufactured Sugars versus Complex Sugars." Aspartame is an artificial non-saccharide sweetener that is marketed under a number of trademark names, including NutraSweet, Equal and Canderel. It is contained in over 6,000 consumer foods and beverages, including (but not limited to) diet sodas and other soft drinks, instant breakfasts, breath mints, cereals, sugar-free chewing gum, cocoa mixes, frozen desserts, gelatin desserts, juices, laxatives, chewable vitamins supplements, milk drinks, pharmaceutical drugs and supplements, shake mixes, tabletop sweeteners, teas, instant coffees, topping mixes, wine coolers and yogurt. Aspartame is a manufactured substance that contains the amino acids aspartic acid and phenylalanine. Phenylalanine is a neurotoxin and can excite the neurons in the brain to the point of cellular death. Phenylalanine is 50% aspartame, and to the degree humans consume diet products, phenylalanine levels are reaching a dangerous peak. ADD/ADHD and emotional and behavioral disorders can all be triggered by too much phenylala-

nine in the diet. In certain markets, aspartame is manufactured using a genetically modified variation of *E.
coli.*[14,15]

It is important to learn about the ingredients
in your foods, especially isolated amino acids such as
phenylalanine. Amino acids are found in combination
in nature for a reason; consumed in isolation they can
have an adverse effect on our health.

4. Juice

"Concentrate" versus "Not from Concentrate." What's
the difference?

a. "Concentrated" juice is made by boiling juice at
high temperatures, which destroys the natural enzymes in the juice. Later some synthetic vitamins
and, in some cases, refined sugar are added back
when the juice is reconstituted.

b. "Not from concentrate" juices are not boiled at
extreme temperatures, nor were essential natural
vitamins destroyed. More often the juices are ob-
tained by squeezing or pressing the fruit, and
most of the enzymes remain intact. Consuming
enzymatically dead food stresses your digestive
system and pancreas. Which one do you want to
drink?

Please read the labels!

Although I do not consume these fatal-four beverages, I am not suggesting that you follow blindly in my footsteps; however, I am encouraging you to be fully aware of the consequences associated with *excesses* so that you can make a conscious and informed decision about your choices. To sum up, these fatal-four beverages, consumed in excess, will create imbalances and weaken your body systems. The question you need to ask yourself is this: Understanding what I have just read, am I willing and prepared to accept the health consequences associated with the excess consumption of these beverages?

Detoxification

Detoxification is one of the most widely used treatments in alternative medicine. It is based on the principle that illnesses are caused by an accumulation of toxic substances (toxins) in the body. One of the secrets to good health is consuming high vibrational, natural/organic nutrient-rich food (what you put in your body); another secret is regular detoxification (what you remove from your body). Did you know that at any given moment, you are carrying 10 to 15 pounds of waste in your intestines? When your body is full of toxins and wastes, it pollutes your blood, organs and cells. As mentioned earlier, these stresses on the internal systems lead to their degeneration. As the vibration frequencies of our internal systems descend, our cell structure begins to mutate (vibration law number two), which eventually leads to DNA damage and disease.

Detoxification can be used as a tool to help relieve symptoms and as a preventative tool to increase overall health, vitality and resistance to disease.

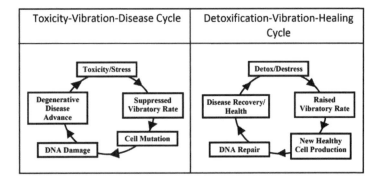

Detox can be helpful for people suffering from many diseases and conditions, including allergies, anxiety, arthritis, asthma, chronic infections, depression, headaches, heart disease, high cholesterol, low blood sugar, digestive disorders, mental illness and obesity.

In addition, detox therapy is helpful to people suffering from immune system disorders such as chronic fatigue syndrome, environmental illness related to multiple chemical sensitivities and fibromyalgia.

With more people becoming aware of environmental pollution, many are turning to detoxification treatments to counteract the detrimental effects of toxins in the environment. Studies show that chemical pollutants such as pesticides, DDT, polychlorinated biphenyls (PCBs) and food additives accumulate in the body. Over-the-counter and prescriptions drugs, as well as recreational drugs and alcohol, also are toxic to the body. The toxins in our food destroy not only antioxidants and cells, but also life force energy (*prana*).

Is there a logical order in which to detox the body?

Yes, there is. If you detox the blood with a clogged liver, where do the toxins go? You must detoxify the liver before you detoxify the blood (and cells throughout the body). Next, if you detoxify the liver, but forget about your toxic colon, it will just get clogged again. Because of our North American diet, our colons are, for the most part, stuffed with toxins that are straining our immune systems.

Therefore, first you detoxify the colon (and we'll work on the kidneys at the same time), then the liver, and then the rest of the body and blood. This is the most intelligent order to follow.

Edgar Cayce developed an acronym to explain his plan to live a healthy life: CARE—circulation, assimilation, relaxation, elimination. Two of these, assimilation and elimination, have to do with your digestive system. With a blood and liver detox, circulation improves, enhancing the pathways for transmitting hormonal messages and communication between the various organs of the immune system. Poor circulation restricts the flow of enzymes that can devour cancer cells. Relaxation, it should be noted, also involves exercise. Exercise and relaxation improve the flow of all systems, and improve liver function.[16]

There are countless elimination and detox remedies readily available in a variety of forms: liquids, powders and capsules. But how do you choose the right detox product for you? Just ask your body by way of muscle testing!

How does muscle testing work? The body has within it and surrounding it an electrical network, or grid. If anything impacts your electrical system that negatively affects your health and your body's balance, your muscles will weaken. This can be demonstrated by having someone apply pressure to your extended arm while your body's electrical system is being adversely impacted; you will find that your arm will not be able to resist the pressure. This is because when the circuits of your electrical system are overloaded, or have short-circuited, your body is weakened. However, if pressure is applied while your electrical system is being positively affected, the circuits remain strong and balanced throughout your body, and your muscles will remain strong and easily resist the pressure being applied.

Note: You will need someone to assist you with this exercise. This exercise will help you determine if a particular detox product would be beneficial to you.

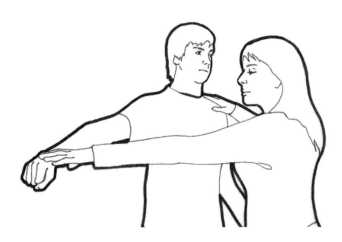

Muscle-Testing Exercise

First, you hold the detox product or herb in one hand, and then extend that arm straight out from your shoulder to your side and parallel to the ground. The person helping you presses down on your extended arm and your opposite shoulder with equal pressure (to facilitate balance). If the detox product or herb is something you need, you'll be able to resist the downward pressure and hold your extended arm rigid. If not, you will not have the muscle power to resist the downward pressure on your arm. The same procedure can also be used to test your body's responses to foods. For example, if you suspect you are allergic to wheat, you can muscle test using a piece of wheat bread, or even a cup of flour. If you are sensitive or allergic to wheat, your arm will weaken under pressure.

pH Balance and Health

Another symptom of toxicity is an unbalanced pH level. Acidity and alkalinity are measured according to the pH (potential of hydrogen) scale. Water, with a pH of 7.0, is considered neutral—neither acid nor alkaline. Any substance with a pH *below* 7.0 is considered acid, becoming more acid as it approaches 1. Any substance with a pH *above* 7.0 is considered alkaline, becoming more alkaline up to a limit of 14.0.

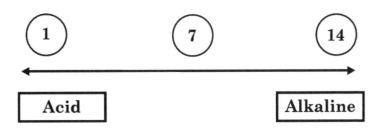

The ideal pH for the human body will vary from individual to individual and compensate for a variety of factors, including blood type, basic personality, energy blocks, education, culture and food. The manner in which people interact with their environment and themselves will influence their pH level. As the above factors change, through building, release, action, frequency and modification, so will the acid-alkaline balance of their body change. In general terms, if your body's pH level falls below 7, this signals that your body is becoming acidic.

You can measure your pH level through either your saliva or urine using pH Hydrion test paper, which you can get at your local pharmacy.

When liquid comes in contact with this pH test paper, it turns a color that corresponds to a chart that comes with the test paper. The chart ranges from blue to yellow, with blue indicating alkaline and yellow indicating acid.

Did you know that your emotions and environment can also affect your pH level? People who are intense and/or passionate tend to exert more influence on their pH balance from day to day than someone less so. The following chart notes the connection between emotional and environmental influences and pH levels.

Emotional and Environmental Influence on pH Levels[17]

Emotion/Environment	Raise or Lower	PH level becomes ...
Hate	Lowers	more acidic
Fear	Lowers	more acidic
Distrust	Lowers	more acidic
Aggressiveness	Raises	more alkaline
Defensiveness	Raises	more alkaline
Meditation	Raises	more alkaline
Reverence	Raises	more alkaline
Peace	Raises	more alkaline
Joy	Raises	more alkaline

You can also change your pH by changing the types of food you eat. For instance, if your pH level is acidic, then you can select and eat foods that are more alkaline in order to regain pH balance. Similarly, if your pH level is alkaline, then select and eat foods that are more acidic to regain pH balance.

Acidifying and Alkalizing Foods

ALKALIZING FOODS

ALKALIZING VEGETABLES	ALKALIZING VEGETABLES
Alfalfa	Onions
Barley Grass	Parsnips
Beets	Peas
Beet Greens	Peppers
Broccoli	Pumpkin
Cabbage	Radishes
Carrot	Rutabaga
Cauliflower	Sea Vegetables
Celery	Spinach
Chard Greens	Spirulina
Chlorella	Sprouts
Collard Greens	Sweet Potatoes
Cucumber	Tomatoes
Dandelion Greens	Watercress
Dulce	Wheat Grass
Edible Flowers	Wild Greens
Eggplant	**ALKALIZING ORIENTAL**
Fermented Vegetables	**VEGETABLES**
Garlic	Maitake
Green Beans	Daikon
Green Peas	Dandelion Root
Kale	Shitake Mushrooms
Kohlrabi	Kombu
Lettuce	Reishi
Mushrooms	Nori
Mustard Greens	Umeboshi
Nightshade Vegetables	Wakame

Acidifying and Alkalizing Foods

ALKALIZING FOODS

ALKALIZING FRUITS
Apple
Apricot
Avocado
Banana
Berries
Blackberries
Cantaloupe
Cherries, sour
Coconut, fresh
Currants
Dates, dried
Figs, dried
Grapes
Grapefruit*
Honeydew Melon
Lemon*
Lime*
Muskmelon
Nectarine*
Orange*
Peach
Pear
Pineapple
Raisins
Raspberries
Rhubarb
Strawberries

ALKALIZING FRUITS
Tangerine*
Tomato
Tropical Fruits
Umeboshi Plums
Watermelon

*Although it might seem that citrus fruits would have an acidifying effect on the body, the citric acid they contain actually has an alkalinizing effect in the system.

ALKALIZING PROTEIN
Almonds
Chestnuts
Millet
Tempeh
Tofu, fermented
Whey Protein Powder

ALKALIZING SWEETENERS
Stevia

ALKALIZING SPICES & SEASONINGS
Cinnamon
Curry
Ginger

Acidifying and Alkalizing Foods

ALKALIZING FOODS

ALKALIZING SPICES & SEASONINGS
Mustard
Chili Pepper
Sea Salt
Miso
Tamari
All Herbs

ALKALIZING MINERALS
Cesium: pH 14
Potassium: pH 14
Sodium: pH 14
Calcium: pH 12
Magnesium: pH 9

ALKALIZING OTHER FOODS
Apple Cider Vinegar
Bee Pollen
Lecithin Granules
Molasses, blackstrap
Probiotic Cultures
Soured Dairy Products
Green Juices
Vegetable Juices
Fresh Fruit Juice
Mineral Water
Alkaline Antioxidant Water

Acidifying and Alkalizing Foods

ACIDIFYING FOODS

ACIDIFYING VEGETABLES
Corn
Lentils
Olives
Winter Squash

ACIDIFYING FRUITS
Blueberries
Canned or Glazed Fruits
Cranberries
Currants
Plums**
Prunes**

> **These fruits leave an alkaline ash but have an acidifying effect on the body.*

ACIDIFYING GRAINS, GRAIN PRODUCTS
Amaranth
Barley
Bran, wheat
Bran, oat
Corn
Cornstarch
Hemp Seed Flour
Kamut
Oats, rolled

ACIDIFYING GRAINS, GRAIN PRODUCTS
Oatmeal
Quinoa
Rice, all
Rice Cakes
Rye
Spelt
Wheat
Wheat Germ
Noodles
Macaroni
Spaghetti
Bread
Crackers, soda
Flour, white
Flour, wheat

ACIDIFYING BEANS & LEGUMES
Black Beans
Chick Peas
Green Peas
Kidney Beans
Lentils
Pinto Beans
Red Beans
Soybeans

Acidifying and Alkalizing Foods

ACIDIFYING FOODS

ACIDIFYING BEANS & LEGUMES

Soy Milk
White Beans
Rice Milk
Almond Milk

ACIDIFYING DAIRY

Butter
Cheese
Cheese, processed
Ice Cream
Ice Milk

ACIDIFYING NUTS & BUTTERS

Cashews
Legumes
Peanuts
Peanut Butter
Pecans
Tahini
Walnuts

ACIDIFYING ANIMAL PROTEIN

Bacon
Beef
Carp

ACIDIFYING ANIMAL PROTEIN

Clams
Cod
Corned Beef
Fish
Haddock
Lamb
Lobster
Mussels
Organ Meats
Oyster
Pike
Pork
Rabbit
Salmon
Sardines
Sausage
Scallops
Shrimp
Scallops
Shellfish
Tuna
Turkey
Veal
Venison

Acidifying and Alkalizing Foods

ACIDIFYING FOODS

ACIDIFYING FATS & OILS
Avocado Oil
Butter
Canola Oil
Corn Oil
Hemp Seed Oil
Flax Oil
Lard
Olive Oil
Safflower Oil
Sesame Oil
Sunflower Oil

ACIDIFYING ALCOHOL
Beer
Spirits
Hard Liquor
Wine

ACIDIFYING OTHER FOODS
Coffee
Vinegar
Mustard
Pepper
Soft Drinks

ACIDIFYING SWEETENERS
Carob
Sugar
Corn Syrup

ACIDIFYING JUNK FOOD
Coca-Cola: pH 2
Beer: pH 2.5
Coffee: pH 4

In addition to using detox products, and eating certain foods, there are some holistic ways to remove toxins from your body and restore pH levels to a balanced and healthy state.

You can detox your body through sweating. Our skin is the largest organ in the body and plays a major role in the detox process. Sweat carries toxins out of the body, pushing them through the pores of the skin.

Some activities to consider to increase sweating include Bikram yoga (or hot yoga), infrared sauna and exercise. Exercise allows the proper flow of body fluids to occur. This in turn stimulates the systems and organs and aids in flushing toxins out of the body.

When engaging in activities that increase sweating, it is critical to replace the water you lose to avoid dehydration. Dehydration is a condition that occurs when the loss of body fluids (mostly water) exceeds the amount of water that is taken in. Symptoms of dehydration in adults include dizziness, dry mouth/swollen tongue, weakness, increased thirst, palpitations (feeling the heart is pounding or jumping), confusion, sluggishness/fainting and decreased urine output or urine color that is deep yellow or amber, to name a few. Keep the body well hydrated with at least four to five quarts (16–20 cups) of *alkaline* water per day when involved in these activities.

Increased sweating also causes certain minerals to be excreted from your pores along with water. Some of these minerals include sodium, potassium, calcium, magnesium and copper. Therefore, it is also essential that you to replace the minerals lost through sweating to avoid mineral deficiency.

Always consult your physician before trying a new therapy or making any change to your regular health regime.

Fasting is another holistic way to remove toxins. The ancient naturopathic healers recognized the natural tendency of people to lose their appetite when they were feeling ill, and therefore imparted the discipline of fasting on a regular basis to promote physical health. Fasting allows the body to eliminate waste material, since it can use the energy that would normally be used to digest food for processing and eliminating waste materials and toxins. There are many fasting programs and methods, and it can be confusing deciding which one to try and for how long. But before you begin any fasting program, I suggest you consult your physician. Fasting is not recommended for everyone. Fasting is contraindicated for pregnant and lactating mothers, for children not yet fully grown (still forming bone and teeth) and for all those suffering serious conditions requiring monitoring by physicians, including people with insulin-dependent type 1 diabetes.

Some benefits of periodic fasting:

- Gives all digestive, assimilative and eliminative organs a much-needed rest.
- Restores and normalizes glandular, metabolic and nervous-system functions.
- Speeds elimination of acid-forming mucus, toxic wastes and dead cells.
- Accelerates new cell and tissue generation.
- Enhances cell oxygenation.

- Vibrationally: Fasting introduces a heightened clarity of consciousness and enhanced innate spirituality, which we often forget we possess.

"True happiness is impossible without true health. True health is impossible without the rigid control of the palate. A genuine fast cleanses the body, mind and soul."
~ Mahatma Gandhi, 1869–1948

Key Message #1:
Several factors contribute to the accumulation of toxins and acid in the body, including our emotional state, environmental factors, ingesting the wrong foods and consuming foods in an improper manner; therefore, a multifaceted approach is required to detox, balance pH levels and promote healing and prevent disease.

Key Message #2:
As you cleanse the body internally and allow the organs, fluids and cells to operate as they were intended, without stress or strain, in harmony and in balance, your energetic body will naturally raise its vibration to resonate with positive internal vibrations. Detoxification is a vital process to counteract internal stress and promote optimal bioelectric flow within and around the body.

Vibration and Mass Media

I remember a time when we lived in a modest old country home. It had a white board-and-batten exterior and a pitched black roof, the basement had an earthen floor and the supporting beam was an actual tree trunk about seven and a half feet high. We had to rent the house for almost a year, while we waited for our new home to be built. The most memorable thing about this house was that it had no cable, no satellite and no TV antenna! When my friends heard that we were renting a house without TV, and we had three children under the age of 11, they were initially astonished. Then there astonishment quickly turned to pity: "Oh you poor thing," I was told. "How will your children survive?" I was asked. "What will you do for entertainment?" they questioned. My humble reply: "We will enjoy each other's company." Some of my fondest memories with our three children are of that summer, when we taught them how to play Monopoly, chess and several other board games. We all went jogging together; in fact, we spent virtually the entire summer outdoors riding bikes, hiking and the like. When the year ended and it was time to move into our new house, we made the monumental family decision to continue to be TV free. Over the following four years, I saw three young children blossom into creative, independent-thinking, well-rounded, loving teenagers. They each discovered new talents and had the time to develop their skills and love of art, poetry, creative writing, filmmaking, music and dance. I often wonder if they would have discovered these hidden talents, and if we would have created so many wonderful memories together, if we had chosen to be entertained or absorbed by TV?

It's safe to say that most of the information we consume via mass media—TV, radio, computer, newspapers—is negative. As described above in the chapter "Thoughts," negative thoughts lower vibration.

When was the last time you heard an uplifting story on the news? When you constantly absorb violent, sensational and negative information, your subconscious mind becomes disturbed and agitated, and negative emotions such as fear, sorrow or pain become elevated. The greater the shock factor in headlines or on radio and TV announcements, the more you want to read or listen to the whole story, and an addictive habit ensues.

How many people do you know who watch TV at night while in bed? In fact, some of those same people are unable to fall asleep without hearing the TV on in the background. It's easy to switch it on and zone out. TV in these cases is used as a pacifier, an electronic babysitter. Watching TV also causes the *thinking* and *creative* part of your brain to shut down. When you watch TV, it is the TV providing you with all the images and messages; TV is doing the work for you. You have only to look at it—no thinking, imagining or creating is involved on your part. Your brain shuts off because it has no job to do. I call this the *brain drain.*

TV also provides some people with a means to escape their own life. They can get lost in the imaginary lives of the characters they watch. If you find yourself watching TV for hours at a time each day, it might be good to think about whether or not you are trying to avoid dealing with some aspect of your life. The continual absorption of negative, sensational and violent media has adverse effects on our brain waves and emotions, which in turn short-circuits or constricts our bioelectric flow (vibration), which reduces our ability to find inner peace and contentment.

Have you noticed that most TV commercials stir up feelings of dissatisfaction and or inferiority? Marketing gurus no longer spend millions trying to convince you to buy their product, instead, they try to convince you that you *will not* be free until you get behind the wheel of such and such car, or that you *will not* find love unless you wear such and such perfume, or that you *cannot* have fun at a party without drinking such and such beverage.

Are you buying what you *don't* really need with money you *don't* really have just to feel better or to fit in? I ask you, whom do you want to feel better than, and what do you want to fit into? Once upon a time you had a cell phone, then you needed a flip cell phone, then you needed a compact mini cell phone, and now you need a PicturePhone/MP3/video/GPS system that fits in your pant pocket!

We live in a consumption-driven society, where we are "programmed" to buy more and spend more. When will it end? It will end when you become consciously aware of your thoughts, emotions and actions and stop being enslaved by them; it will end when you begin to reflect on what is truly important so that you can regain balance, peace and joy in your life.

Key Message:
Excess consumption of mass media can drain your positive energy and replace it with feelings of fear, hopelessness, dissatisfaction and inadequacy. These negative emotions suppress your vibrational levels by creating mental agitation, which leads to stress, which eventually leads to disease.

Vibration Exercise: Media Deprogramming
For the next 30 days, don't turn on the TV or read the newspaper. Notice how you feel in the evening before falling asleep, and in the morning when you wake up. Notice any changes in what or who you are dreaming about. Observe the change in your mood or attitude throughout the day. Best of all, notice how much more *time* you gain to do other activities, such as connecting more with family and friends, reading a book you have been putting off for a while or resurrecting a hobby that you either lost interest in or lost the time to do!

Brain Waves-Stress-Health Connection

Our brain is made up individual cells called *neurons*. These neurons communicate with each other by electrical changes—which we can see in the form of brain waves as shown on an EEG (electroencephalogram). To measure brain waves, electrodes are placed on the scalp using an electroencephalograph. Brain waves are measured in cycles per seconds or Hertz (Hz for short). The lower the number of Hz, the slower the brain activity.

There are four basic brain waves: *beta, alpha, theta* and *delta*, which are linked to different states of brain functioning and different states of consciousness. Each of the four brain waves is good for some activities; however, we can become imbalanced or stressed by overstimulating some brain wave states and ignoring or suppressing others. For instance, if we cannot turn on theta or delta brain waves, we can suffer from insomnia, restlessness and impatience.

Beta Brain Waves

Beta brain waves occur between 14 and 30 Hz, but

during intense mental activity, they can reach 50 Hz; that is, beta waves characterize the conscious waking state at 14 cycles per second and up.

Beta waves occur in individuals who are attentive and alert to external stimuli or exert specific mental effort. Beta waves also occur during deep sleep and rapid eye movement (REM) sleep, when the eyes move rapidly in different directions. Beta brain waves represent excitement of the cortex to a higher state of alertness or tension.

Alpha Brain Waves

Alpha brain waves occur at a lower cycle, between 8 and 13 Hz. In general, the alpha rhythm is the prominent EEG wave pattern of an adult who is awake but relaxed with eyes closed.

When we relax and clear our mind of wandering thoughts, our brain generates alpha waves. In the alpha state, one is open to suggestion, as the conscious logical mind is subdued.

Psychic experiences can happen in the alpha state. Both daydreaming and sleep dreaming occur while in the alpha state.

Theta Brain Waves

Theta brain waves occur between 4 and 7 Hz. When you are daydreaming, fantasizing, imagining, coming up with ideas or practicing inspirational thinking, your brain generates theta brain waves.

Although it is possible to have psychic experiences in

the alpha state, the most thoughtful experiences occur at the theta level. If you drive for a long while on a straight road, you can go into theta state.

The theta level opens the door to falling even deeper into the psychic/astral world. At this level, you are able to experience astral travel and psychic communication, achieve enlightenment and enter into other dimensions.

Delta Brain Waves

Delta brain waves occur below 3.5 Hz; that is, brain wave activity in the delta state ranges from 0 to 4 cycles per second. This is total unconsciousness or deep, dreamless sleep. When we are asleep and not dreaming, the brain generates delta waves.

Brain Waves and the Stress Scenario

Does this sound familiar? You wake up suddenly out of a deep sleep (delta brain waves) to an alarm. Then you immediately feel stress and anxiety (beta brain waves) about the time and being late. After insufficient sleep, you pour caffeine down your throat to force yourself into wakefulness, and the caffeine suppresses theta and alpha brain waves, while promoting beta brain waves. All day you work under the stress of deadlines and other pressures (beta, beta, and more beta), until at night you fall exhausted into deep sleep (delta brain waves), having spent too little time unwinding, relaxing and drowsing (which would have given you a bit more theta and alpha brain waves). This stressful cycle shifts your brain suddenly and forcefully from delta to beta and back to delta.[18]

So how can you feel less stressed? To decrease feelings of stress and anxiety, try to increase your alpha brain wave activity. This may also improve the strength of your immune system, since stress can weaken it. Other benefits of increasing alpha brain waves include increased creativity and ability to reach peak performance in athletic activity. High alpha people are also less hostile, less angry and less depressed. High alpha people are also friendlier, more vigorous, more motivated and more clear thinking. Which waves do you want to surf today?

Alpha Wave Activities to Consider

You can stimulate alpha brain waves using a number of activities, techniques and methods, including meditation, yoga, drumming, chanting, belly breathing and using high-vibration sound instruments such as Tibetan singing bowls, crystal quartz singing bowls, EEG biofeedback and brainwave entrainment, to name a few.

> **Morning Exercise: Wake Up Gradually**
> If you have a radio alarm clock, consider switching from the alarm setting, which shocks your brain into beta mode, and set it instead to a radio station or CD that plays soothing music or sounds of nature. This will ease your transition from delta (deep sleep) into theta, followed by alpha (relaxed and eyes opening) and finally into beta mode (eyes opened, stretching and starting your day).

Bedtime Exercise: Wind Down Gradually
There is a yoga pose that you can easily do from the comfort of your bed that will completely relax your nervous system, and wind down the brain waves from beta to alpha, and with practice even get you to a theta state. The yoga pose is called *Shavasana* (sometimes written as *Savasana*) or *Corpse pose*. It is a relaxing posture intended to rejuvenate your body, mind and spirit. While Shavasana is a good way to reduce stress and tension, it is not recommended for meditation as it has the tendency to induce sleepiness.

1. Lie on your back, spread your arms and legs about 45 degrees from the sides of your body. Tilt your head slightly back so it rests comfortably (no pillow required). Make sure you are warm and comfortable.

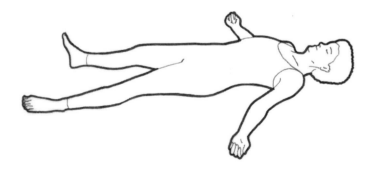

2. Close your eyes. Begin to inhale slowly through your nostrils and allow the air to fill your belly (your belly rises as you inhale), then slowly exhale softly through your mouth without any force (your belly falls as you exhale). Allow your entire body to become soft and heavy. As you relax, feel your whole body rising and falling with each breath.

3. Scan your body from your toes to your fingers to the crown of your head, looking for or sensing any areas of tightness and contracted muscles. Consciously release and relax any areas that you find tense.

4. Release all control of your breath, your mind and your body. Allow your body to move deeper and deeper into a state of total relaxation.

5. Try to stay in Shavasana for 20 to 30 minutes.

6. Remain where you are and gently fall asleep, or release this yoga pose by slowly deepening your breath, wiggling your fingers and toes, reaching your arms over your head and stretching your whole body. Exhale while bending your knees into your chest and roll over to one side, coming into a fetal position. When you are ready, slowly inhale and come up to a seated position.

These are some of the benefits of this relaxing pose:

- A decrease in heart rate and the rate of respiration.
- A decrease in blood pressure.
- A decrease in muscle tension.
- A shift into alpha and sometimes theta brain waves.
- A reduction in anxiety.
- A reactivation of the natural biorhythms of the physical and subtle body.
- An improvement in concentration and in memory.
- A decrease in fatigue, coupled with deeper and sounder sleep.
- Improved self-confidence.

Breath Work

Our life begins with a breath and ends with a breath. To breathe is to be alive! The relationship between the flow of energy and breath is recognized in many cultures around the world. The energy, or subtle, body can be influenced and transformed using specific breathing techniques. Through breath, vital energy enters the *chakras* (energy centers that connect our psychic and physical energy systems), *nadis* (channels for the flow of *prana*) and *aura* (an energy field of subtle luminous radiation that surrounds all living things). This flow of energy also animates the physical body.

In the yogic system, breathing exercises are called *pranayama*; *prana* means "vital energy" and *yama* means "control." Therefore, in yoga, to breathe is to control vital energy!

Rhythmic breathing is a great exercise for relaxation and oxygenating the body. The yogis say that rhythmic-breathing exercises allow the body to reestablish its own natural rhythm and attune us more to the cosmic rhythm. Deep rhythmic-breathing exercises also allow the body to absorb much more oxygen, which is vital to the purity and health of our blood, organs and cells. This form of breathing also promotes optimal resonance in the overall vibration of our energetic body, and enables us to release latent powers and untapped human potential.

Similar to the relationship between sweating and detox, there is a relationship between breathing and detox. Breathing draws oxygen into the lungs. The oxygen—which is absorbed by the hemoglobin in the blood and transferred to every cell in the body—provides life and energy to our cells while detoxifying our blood and transferring vital nutrients to our organs and cells. However, if insufficient quantities of fresh air reach the lungs, the blood cannot be purified, and consequently the body is robbed of sufficient nourishment, and the internal waste products that should have been destroyed and excreted are returned to the circulation, toxifying the entire system, depleting the body of life force energy and triggering disease. When the immune system is compromised by a lack of oxygen, the body is more vulnerable to bacterial, viral and parasitic infections and colds and flus. In order to regain health, the body must obtain sufficient oxygen to revitalize energy and cleanse itself of toxic substances.

According to Yogi Yamacharaka in *Hindu-Yogi Science of Breath*,[19] "when it is remembered that the greater portion of prana acquired by man comes from the air inhaled, the importance of proper breathing is readily understood."

Following are suggested breathing exercises to promote relaxation, increase oxygen intake, increase prana flow and calm the central nervous system. For all these exercises, it is important to sit in a comfortable meditative position (i.e., with your back straight, your feet planted firmly on the floor and your hands resting on your lap) and to be in a place where you will not be disturbed for at least 15 minutes.

Rhythmic Belly-Breathing Exercise
Belly breathing, or abdominal breathing, massages the internal organs and develops life force energy. This exercise is done in a ratio of 1:1:1. To begin, use a count of four.
   1. Inhale slowly for a count of four.
   2. Hold your breath for a count of four.
   3. Exhale slowly for a count of four.
As your progress and concentration improves, gradually increase to a count of six, then eight. Breathe in through your nostrils, with your mouth closed, and allow the abdomen to expand like a balloon. Breathe out through your nostrils with your mouth closed, and pull your stomach in toward your spine. This exercise allows the natural life force in the air around you to be rhythmically supplied to your body and nervous system.

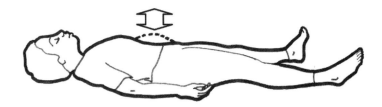

**Alternate Nostril-Breathing
(*Anuloma Viloma*) Exercise**

This is a powerful pranayama. As the name suggests, it alternates the flow of breath/prana through one nostril then the other. Yogis realize that through intense practice it is possible to balance the negative and positive flow of energy, thus creating neutral energy. This breathing exercise has several benefits, including

- balancing the autonomic nervous system,
- balancing the left and right hemispheres of the brain,
- improving concentration,
- purifying the *nadis* (channels of prana flow),
- aligning the individual force field with the universal force field and
- optimizing the vibratory rate of the entire physical system.

It is recommended that this practice be done in a ratio of 1:4:2. For example, inhale for a count of two, then hold for eight, and release for a count of four. You will place your left middle and index fingers in your right palm, creating a *Vishnu mudra* (specific hand gesture that directs energy), and you will block your right nostril with your right thumb, and the left nostril with the remaining fingers of your right hand.

continued on next page

Alternate Nostril-Breathing
(*Anuloma Viloma*) Exercise *continued*
The six stages to complete a round of alternate
nostril breathing are as follows:

1. Block the right nostril, inhale through the left.
2. Hold the breath, block both nostrils.
3. Block the left nostril, exhale through the right.
4. Inhale through the right, block the left.
5. Hold the breath, block both nostrils.
6. Block the right nostril, exhale through the left.

Repeat between three and seven times. Increase
the count as your practice and concentration
improve.

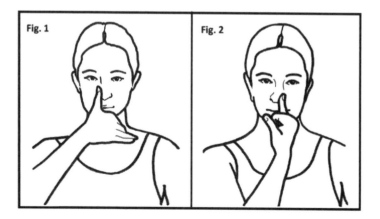

Vitalizing-Breath Exercise

In order to accomplish the vitalizing breath, all three parts of your lungs—the lower, middle and upper—must be filled. You fill your lungs as a glass of water is filled—from the bottom up. The lungs are then emptied as a glass of water—from the top down.

1. Sit or stand erect and relaxed.
2. Inhale as much air as possible through your nostrils, drawing it down into your lower lungs just above the diaphragm in a continual flow of incoming air. The entire inhalation should be a smooth, even intake of air into your lungs without any stops or jerks.
3. Fill your middle lung, expanding your rib cage as much as possible without straining. At the completion of the inhalation, your midsection should be drawn in a little while holding your breath.
4. Fill your upper lungs.
5. At the end of the breath, lift your shoulders a little and take one last inhalation of air into your lungs.
6. Hold your breath for a few counts, but not to the point of discomfort.
7. Exhale through your mouth with your lips pursed slightly. Do not blow the air out forcefully. This step is especially important as it sets up resistance to the exhalation, which enables the energizing of your physical body and the storage of prana in your subtle body.

Key Message:
Breath work allows the body to obtain adequate oxygen, which is vital to the purity and health of our blood, cells and organs. Oxygen regulates all our bodily functions, energizes our cells so they can regenerate, metabolizes our food and eliminates toxins and wastes through oxidation.

Breath work is also essential for increasing prana (life force energy), cleansing, rejuvenating and balancing our energetic bodies and systems (chakras, nadis, aura, meridians), which improves our capacity to raise our vibratory rates to their optimal frequency.

Essential Oils

Essential oils are the natural volatile oils that are extracted from the aromatic essences of certain plants, shrubs, flowers, trees and herbs. They contain virtually all of the plants' nutrients, and their vibrational frequency is compatible and beneficial to human vibrational frequency.

Modern medicine has recently rediscovered what the ancients already discovered over 10,000 years ago—that essential oils provide us with oxygen (i.e., improve human cell function) and increase our vibrational frequency, which in turn boosts our immune function and strengthens our defenses against bacteria, viruses and disease. Today, essential oils are valued as a treatment for improving physical and emotional health.

Essential oils (EOs) are not used internally, but are inhaled or applied to the skin. Clinical research shows that these concentrated oils have the highest vibrational frequency of any natural substance known to man. Furthermore, EOs produce the highest level of oxygenating molecules of any substance currently known to man. Why is this important for our health and well-being? Because bacteria cannot live in an oxygen-rich, high-vibrational environment! (Vibration law # 1.)

Essential Oils and Health

Clinical research has proven that 100% pure essential oils to have immune-stimulating, antiviral, anti-infection, anti-bacterial, antimicrobial, antiseptic, antitumoral and antifungal properties.[20]

Because of the high vibrational level and identity structure of EOs (i.e., they have high oxygenating activity and contain negative ions and ozone), they can push toxins out of our cells and pull potassium and other vital nutrients back into our cells. They naturally balance and normalize human cell function and restore diseased and malnourished cells back to health.

Some Essential Oils and Their Corresponding Frequency[21]

Essential Oil	Hz
Angelica	85
Basil	52
Chamomile	105
Juniper	98
Lavender	118
Myrrh	105
Peppermint	78
Ravensara	134
Rose	320
Sandalwood	96

Note: The frequencies of essential oils vary according to each batch, growing conditions, weather and soil conditions.

How to use essential oils to raise your personal vibration is further explained later in the chapter "Vibration Work with Essential Oils."

The Chakra-Vibration-Health Connection

Chakra means "wheel of light" in Sanskrit, and refers to cone-shaped vortices that spin and vibrate within the energy body. The chakras are energy centers that draw energy from the universal energy field and distribute it out into the energy pathways, known as *nadis* in the traditional Indian yogic system, or *meridians* in the traditional Chinese healing system—and from here energy radiates out into the *aura*.

Ancient cultures throughout the world believe that people exist, not as solid matter, but as vibrational beings in direct contact with a greater source of energy surrounding us. Energy takes many forms, from the finer forms of *prana* (vital energy) to the denser forms of the physical body and the material universe. The chakra system, therefore, is a model for the flow of energy that runs through all life and influences our physical, emotional and mental states.

If a situation occurs to impede the flow of life energy (i.e., stress; toxicity and mental, emotional and physical disturbances), the *chakras* (wheels of light) slow down activity, and the energy becomes sluggish and even stagnant or blocked. If the situation is temporary, the energy will resume to its natural flow. However, if the situation persists for a length of time, the chakras will need stimulation to become active again and spin at an optimal rate. There are various ways to stimulate and rebalance the chakras using the vibrational exercises described in the next three chapters.

Below is a diagram of the seven major chakras followed by a chart that depicts the relationship between these major chakras, their associated body parts, glands, psychological states and emotions.

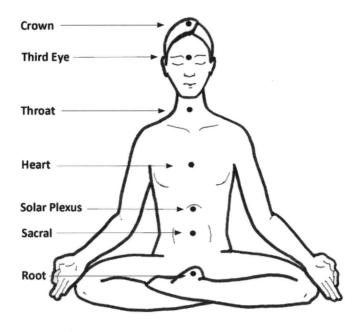

Crown
Third Eye
Throat
Heart
Solar Plexus
Sacral
Root

The Seven Major Chakras

Major Chakra	Gland	Body Part	Psychological Statement	Emotional States (balanced/ unbalanced)
Root	Adrenal cortex	Feet, legs, bones, spine	I have (a physical body)	Safe/fearful Secure/rigid Excitement/ restriction Alive/lethargic
Sacral	Ovaries/ testes	Womb, genitals, kidney, bladder, muscles	I can	Express emotions easily/ pent up emotions
Solar plexus	Pancreas	Stomach, small intestines, liver, gallbladder, spleen	I feel	Joy/uncaring Laughter/ unfeeling Conflict/ depression Happiness/ quick tempered
Heart	Thymus	Heart, lungs, arms, hands	I love	Unconditional love/ conditional love

The Seven Major Chakras

Major Chakra	Gland	Body Part	Psychological Statement	Emotional States (balanced/ unbalanced)
Throat	Thyroid	Throat, ears, mouth	I speak/ I hear	Stillness/ restlessness Peaceful/ anxious
Third eye	Pituitary	Left/right cerebral hemispheres, mind function	I see/ I know	Intelligence/ mental dullness
Crown	Pineal	Top of the skull and beyond; transcends the physical body	I am (Divine)	Peace/ constant worry Oneness/ fragmented

Vibration Work
with Essential Oils

Essential oils (EOs) carry high vibration frequencies and are regarded as the life force of plants, and therefore communicate directly with the life force of humans. They possess a harmonic direct current (DC) frequency that is compatible and harmonic with the electrical field of the human body. When molecules of EOs are inhaled or applied to the skin, they resonate with your body tissues in a natural harmonic manner. This resonance stimulates your own natural frequency and begins to restore coherence to your bioelectric fields to produce healing and maintain wellness.

Many ancient cultures used aromatics for healing, removing evil spirits, raising consciousness, protection, purification, ritual and pleasure. The term *evil spirits* is used collectively to include all manner of negative energies, negative thoughts and physical disease.

Vibration Work

Select the appropriate essential oil and blend it with a *carrier* seed oil such as almond, jojoba or grape seed oil. The blend should be in the ratio of 5 drops of essential oil to 4 teaspoons (20 mL) of carrier oil. Prepare small quantities at a time, as some essential oils can quickly destabilize or go rancid. Small amounts of the mixture can be rubbed on those areas of the body, or chakras, requiring attention. You can also combine meditation or breath work while working with essential oils to facilitate raising your vibration higher while clearing those stagnant or blocked energies.

Note: Essential oils should not be used during pregnancy unless under the supervision of a qualified aroma therapist. Essential oils have the ability to absorb into the body and cells within minutes.

Essential Oils for Balancing Chakras

Major Chakra	Body Part	Beneficial Essential Oil
Root	Feet, legs, bones, spine	Patchouli, cypress, vetivert
Sacral	Womb, genitals, kidney, bladder, muscles	Clary sage, jasmine, rose, ylang ylang, sandalwood
Solar plexus	Stomach, small intestines, liver, gallbladder, spleen	Rosemary, juniper, geranium, peppermint, ginger, black pepper, citrus oils
Heart	Heart, lungs, arms, hands	All floral oils, angelica, palmarosa
Throat	Throat, ears, mouth	Frankincense, chamomile, sandalwood
Third eye	Left/right cerebral hemispheres, mind function	Frankincense, sandalwood, benzoin, amber, myrrh
Crown	Top of the skull and beyond; transcends the physical body and controls the esoteric anatomy	Lavender, bay laurel, hyacinth, valerian

Vibration Work with Gems and Crystals

Gems and crystals are gifts from Mother Earth. Crystals can amplify thought vibrations and positive vibrations and create healing. They also act as channels for healing by drawing out negative, low vibrations, and bringing in positive, higher vibrations in the auric field, chakras and the energy systems, which ultimately improves the physical body.

Gems and crystals need to be cleansed and charged before personal use. They also need to be cleansed when they have been worn for some time. Here are a few ways you can cleanse and charge crystals:

- Air. Use a smudge stick made from sage, sweet grass, cedar and/or lavender; light it, and once it is smoking well, put out the flames and let the smoke rise up over the crystals.
- Water. Hold your crystal under running cold water (avoid chemically treated tap water), or soak them overnight in sea-salt water. Caution: Do not soak gemstones that are porous such as lapis lazuli, turquoise, malachite or amber.

- Earth. Bury your crystals in earth or sand for 24 to 48 hours.
- Fire. Place your crystals in sunlight for 3 to 4 hours.
- Breathe/Intention. Place the stone in the center of one hand, and then bring your hands together as in prayer, placing your hands in front of your mouth. Hold the thought or say, "I cleanse and clear this stone so it can be used for healing." Blow sharply through your hands, and then hold the thought or say, "So be it."

Vibration Work

Gems and crystals can be worn around the neck, placed over the body or placed on the chakras. The length of time you wear or use one is determined by your own inner wisdom and guidance. When healing is complete, it is important to cleanse the gem or crystal, as it will have absorbed the negativity discharged from the chakra. (Please see the method above for cleansing gems and crystals.)

Gems and Crystals for Balancing Chakras

Major Chakra	Body Part	Beneficial Gems and Crystals
Root	Feet, legs, bones, spine	Red jasper, garnet, smoky quartz, obsidian, ruby, black star sapphire, red jade
Sacral	Womb, genitals, kidney, bladder, muscles	Carnelian, amber, orange calcite, coral
Solar plexus	Stomach, small intestines, liver, gallbladder, spleen	Citrine, tiger eye, topaz
Heart	Heart, lungs, arms, hands	Rose quartz, green tourmaline, emerald, green jade, green aventurine, pink carnelian
Throat	Throat, ears, mouth	Blue lace agate, lapis lazuli, blue quartz, turquoise, lazulite
Third eye	Left/right cerebral hemispheres, mind function	Sapphire, lapis lazuli, sodalite, jet, black opal, azurite
Crown	Top of the skull and beyond; transcends the physical body and controls the esoteric anatomy	Amethyst, diamond, selenite, clear quartz, pearl

Vibration Work with Sound and Color

Everything is made up of electromagnetic energy vibrating at different frequencies that correspond to sound, light and color. Both color and sound healing therapies have been used for thousands of years in most ancient cultures throughout the world, and they are combined in this chapter.

Color healing, known as *chromotherapy*, can be implemented in a number of ways. In ancient times, great halls were built specifically for color healing, where individuals were bathed in light that was filtered through various colored glass panels or windows. The origins of healing with color can be traced back to ancient Egypt and Greece.

During the early twentieth century, investigations into the therapeutic use of color were carried out in Europe, most notably by the Austrian philosopher Rudolf Steiner, who related color to form, shape and sound. He suggested that the vibrational quality of certain colors is amplified by some forms, and that certain combinations of color and shape have either destructive or regenerative effects on living organisms.

Rudolf Steiner's work was continued by Theo Gimbel,

who established the Hygeia Studios and College of Colour Therapy in Britain. A colleague named Max Lüscher, a former professor of psychology at Basel University in Switzerland, claimed that color preferences demonstrate states of mind and/or glandular imbalance, and can be used for physical and psychological diagnosis.

With respect to vibration work, the principle idea of color healing is to match the color to its associated chakra, or associated body part(s), that needs rebalancing or healing, as indicated on the chart on page 107, "Sound and Color for Balancing Chakras." Different colors can be used to stimulate or sedate a chakra. For example, when a chakra (energy centre) is blocked with too much energy, it needs to be cleared and soothed by releasing some of that energy (sedation); when a chakra is depleted or low in energy, then it needs energy transferred in or stimulation to allow the energy to move (i.e., spin) at an optimal rate. Using color is just one of the ways that our energy can be transformed.

The color chart on the following pages can provide insight for you to explore the reasons why you may be attracted to certain colors and not attracted to others.[22]

Color Chart

Color	Preference for Color	Aversion to Color
Red	Red is associated with passionate love, sex, great energy, impulse, action and stimulation, assertiveness and aggression, courage, strength and power, adventure, danger, warnings, revolt and revolution. Temperamental and ambitious people with a need for personal freedom.	A person who has an aversion to red may be overactive, too impulsive, hot-tempered, aggressive and egocentric, or have difficulties with people with such characteristics. It can also symbolize deeply hidden fears and rejection of his or her own assertiveness.
Orange	Orange represents the warmth of the fire. It brings even more energy than yellow; it represents celebration and great abundance, comfort, enjoyment of the senses. Warm, sociable, dynamic and independent people who dedicate themselves to whatever they do.	A person who has an aversion to orange may have suppressed sexual feelings or other difficulties with sensual enjoyment of life. The attitude can also be oversensual, indulgent or too materialistic.

Color Chart

Color	Preference for Color	Aversion to Color
Green	Green brings peace, rest, hope, comfort and nurturing, calmness and harmony. Interest in nature, plants, fellow humans, children and animals, health and healing, natural and plain life. Longing for a safe home and family life. A dislike of conflicts.	A person who has an aversion to green may be more interested in independence and self-development than in a warm family life. May prefer to keep a certain distance in (sexual) relationships.
Blue	Cool and soothing, dreamy and magical. Peace and rest. For people who keep a certain distance, but give calm and practical help; they are faithful and loyal, have a sense for order, logic and rational thinking. Flying in day dreaming, ideals or nostalgia when felt misunderstood. Dark blue is more severe and can be melancholic. Blue is also the color of truth.	A person who has an aversion to blue may be very disciplined, be a strong career worker or have an aversion to commentary or restriction. He or she may have charted out a clear direction to follow for his or her life.

Color Chart

Color	Preference for Color	Aversion to Color
Violet/ Purple	Colors for meditation, contemplation, mysticism, spirituality and religious power. A longing to ascend and dissolve polarities (purple consists of the active red and passive blue) to improve the world. Reservation, mystery and dignity. Soft, sensitive people with often paranormal abilities.	A person who has an aversion for violet/purple may have very serious attitude toward life and may find it difficult to give dreams, fantasies, vague fears or memories a place in it. May have a tendency to reject everything he or she regards as unnatural or unrealistic.

Sound and Color for Balancing Chakras

Major Chakra	Color	Musical Note	Seed Sound
Root	Red	Low C	Lam
Sacral	Orange	D	Vam
Solar plexus	Yellow	E	Ram
Heart	Green, rose pink	F	Yam
Throat	Light blue	G	Ham
Third eye	Indigo	A	Aum
Crown	Violet	B	Om

Vibration Work with Color

There are several ways to work with color for healing. You can wear the appropriate colors or colored gemstones for healing, or bathe in colored water—you can buy non-toxic color therapy bath products at many holistic stores. You can use floodlights with colored filters so colored light absorbs through your subtle body/aura and skin. You can also lay your hands on the chakra or associated body part, and using visualization, mentally direct specific color rays into the chakra and body for self-healing. I encourage you to exercise your body's innate intelligence to guide you to select a color(s) that is most beneficial to you at this time. Similar to choosing what color clothes you want to wear, allow your intuition to guide you to the color you are most attracted to.

Sound and Healing

Sound healing is the educated and conscious use of audible vibrational frequencies to help us manifest higher levels of health and well-being.

Sound healing is founded on the premise that all matter is vibrating at specific frequencies. And as such, sound is a powerful tool because it is vibrational in nature, and we are vibrational beings. In fact, quantum physicists define the human body as vibrating strings of energy. In other words, matter is nothing more than energy vibrating at different frequencies, giving us the illusion of density. Sound can be used to energize or sedate our physical body, transform our emotional and mental states and expand or alter our consciousness.

Sound as a healing modality is found in most ancient

cultures and religions, and is believed to be the oldest form of healing. The creative and transformational power of sound is known in many cultures around the world that share a common belief that sound is the prime organizing force of all matter and creation in our known universe.

Edgar Cayce once said, "Sound will be the medicine of the future." Now in the twenty-first century, we have a new sound medicine called *sonocytology*. Sonocytology is the study of the sound of healthy cells as compared with the sound of mutated or diseased cells. Research and trials are underway to study how the sound of healthy cells of an organ can reharmonize, reenergize and reprogram the mutated cells of the same organ and restore that organ to a healthy state. This new medical breakthrough, using audible sound medicine, may offer the greatest potential for non-invasive healing.

In this century, as we seem to be moving further and further away from natural environments and natural biorhythms, high vibration sound, with its pure and unbiased simplicity, offers us a link back to that which we knew before modern advances and technologies separated us from nature.

Sound Vibration Work with Voice

Our voices are the oldest sound instruments on the planet! We can use our voices to tone, chant and sing, and for repeating mantras, affirmations and prayers to manifest healing, improve our mood, raise our consciousness and increase our vibratory rate. I encourage you to explore the multitude of sound CDs specifically designed to assist you with vocal toning, chanting and mantras.

Sound Vibration Work with Instruments

Certain instruments are known to induce alpha and theta brain wave states, which are required to begin or accelerate healing, dissolving energy blocks and raising one's vibratory rate. These instruments include drums, Tibetan singing bowls, quartz crystal singing bowls, harp, monochord, tambura (South India) and tanpura (North India), to name a few. You can listen to these instruments on a music CD, participate in a sound circle or enjoy a live musical performance.

Sound Vibration Work with Entrainment

The sensation of auditory binaural beats occurs when two coherent sounds of similar frequencies are presented to each ear with stereo headphones or speakers. If the left ear is presented with a steady tone of 200 Hz, and the right ear a steady tone of 210 Hz, these two tones combine in the brain. The brain integrates the two frequencies, producing a sensation of a third sound called the *binaural beat*. If binaural frequencies are applied to the brain, it becomes possible to entrain the brain frequency from one stage to another (i.e., from beta to alpha to theta to delta). The result is a focused, whole-brain state known as *hemispheric synchronization*, or *Hemi-Sync*, where the left and right hemispheres work together in a state of coherence.

Some benefits of brain wave entrainment include reduced stress, increased ability to learn, improved memory and brain function, ability to enter deep meditative states easily and ability to unleash your intuitive and psychic powers.

Brain Wave Maps:

Before and After Hemispheric Synchronization

Incoherent brain-wave pattern with limited thought processes	Coherent brain-wave pattern - enhanced whole-brain potential

Spend Time in Nature

On a typical day, we move from a building, usually our home, to some form of transportation, a car, taxi, bus, train or school bus, to yet another building, our school or work place, unless we are fortunate to work outdoors for at least part of the day, or young enough to enjoy recess breaks at school.

With urban sprawl, shrinking of green spaces and open spaces, fear of "stranger-danger" limiting children's play-time, the convenience of drive-thru and online services and the emerging culture of techno-obsessed people of all ages, North Americans are suffering from nature deprivation.

Nature deprivation is the disconnection of humanity from the natural biorhythms that assist in stimulating and maintaining our own physical biorhythms and providing us with life force energy, or *prana*. Nature provides us with an abundance of life force energy (i.e., nutrient-rich natural/raw foods, sunshine, fresh air, earth and the cosmos), which is a key component to our physical and spiritual health.

To quote the renowned naturalist and essayist John Burroughs (1837–1921), "I go to nature to be soothed and healed, and to have my senses put in order."

And while you may be thinking, "I don't have time to

go for a stroll. I have too much to do," consider this, if you don't *take* the time, then how can you ever *have* the time? It all boils down to choice and priority.

Here are a few reasons why you should make the great outdoors a part of your daily life:

1. We Need Sunshine

Medical studies around the world have shown that sunlight, through its action on the skin, enhances the production of vitamin D_3, which is an important form of vitamin D that prevents many chronic diseases, including breast, colon and prostate cancers; osteoporosis; high blood pressure; hypertension and heart disease; seasonal affective disorder (SAD); premenstrual syndrome (PMS); depression; multiple sclerosis (MS); type 1 diabetes; rheumatoid arthritis; psoriasis and obesity.

Exposure to sunlight increases "feel-good" endorphins and acts as a natural antidepressant. Very few foods naturally contain vitamin D; sunlight supplies most of our of vitamin D requirement. We need adequate vitamin D for cellular health, bone health, organ health, mental health and weight management.

How much sunshine do you need? That depends primarily on your geography and how much melanin is in your skin. Living in northern latitudes, especially in winter, can lead to vitamin D deficiency and sometimes depression from lack of sun exposure.

People with darker skin have the ability to stay in the sun much longer than fairer-skinned people because of the higher amount of melanin in their skin, but that also means that it takes much longer for them to produce the needed amount of vitamin D; it may take as much as a half to one full hour of sunshine to do the trick. Lighter-skinned people have a lot less melanin in their skin and need minimal exposure to the sun, sometimes only 10 to 15 minutes per day to get adequate vitamin D.

2. We Need Trees to Provide Fresh Air

Trees provide a natural exchange of fresh oxygen for carbon monoxide. Breathing air into and out of your lungs brings in oxygen and gets rid of carbon dioxide. This is also referred to as a carbon cycle—one of many of the biorhythms of nature.

In the carbon cycle, plants absorb carbon dioxide from the atmosphere and use it, combined with water they get from the soil, to make the nutrients they need for growth. The process of photosynthesis converts the carbon atoms from carbon dioxide into sugars. The carbon becomes part of the energy system for ecosystems. To fuel our body, we inhale oxygen from the environment and use it to oxidize carbohydrates to release energy, the reverse process of photosynthesis. The process in which this energy is made available for growth and other activities is called respiration, and produces carbon dioxide, which is released from our body through the lungs.

Life force prana is also absorbed into the body by the lungs during breathing. (Please see the chapter "Breath Work" above for exercises to increase prana.)

3. More Reasons to Love Trees

Trees increase our quality of life by bringing natural elements and wildlife habitat into urban settings. Trees help slow global climate change; for example, urban trees help offset climate change by capturing atmospheric carbon dioxide in their tissues, reducing energy used by buildings and reducing carbon dioxide emissions from fossil fuel-based power plants. There is growing evidence that trees help reduce air pollutants that can trigger asthma and other respiratory illnesses. Green spaces also encourage physical activity—a healthy habit for all of us!

4. We Need to Connect to the Earth

Being in nature connects us to the earth, and grounds us as we walk. Being surrounded by other living beings, both large and small, reminds us that we human beings are simply one form of life on this great ball we call Planet Earth. Respect and enjoyment of nature can lead us to a sense of spirituality and appreciation for powers more intelligent and larger than ourselves.

Spending time connecting with nature nourishes the soul, reminding us that we are never truly alone. Nature speaks to us every moment, if we choose to listen. When we tune into the sounds of nature, we receive messages that have the power to uplift us, energize us and transform us.

Vibration Exercise: Reconnecting to Mother Earth

When was the last time you walked barefoot outside? Weather permitting, I invite you to slip off your shoes and feel the sand, earth or long grass caress your toes. Let the energy flow into your feet and embrace you. Be aware of your breath as you walk, and as you inhale, visualize Mother Earth's loving energies and prana drawing into your hands and arms, feet and legs. As you exhale, release those energies and thoughts that no longer serve your greatest good.

How to Spend More Time in Nature

First and foremost, unplug from any wired or wireless device you use or carry around with you; they are the antithesis of relaxation, peace and freedom!

Now open the door and ...

Take a stroll in the park, garden or designated forest trail, or hike through the mountains. Go camping or enjoy an outdoor sport while getting fresh air and sunshine. Or simply lie back in a comfortable hammock among the flowers and trees in your backyard!

More than 100 research studies show that direct contact with nature reduces stress, increases our creative energy, improves problem-solving abilities and enhances self-discipline. Enjoying the beauty of nature also gives us a sense of connection and belonging and a broader sense of community.

Spend Time in Silence and Meditation

As mentioned earlier, for healing to occur the mind has to reach a state of relaxation, peacefulness or contentment to allow positive thoughts to flow with ease and allow vibrational frequencies to increase. This silent practice is known to develop strength of will, clarity, patience and inner peace.

One of the ways to cultivate a mental state of peacefulness is through silence. The regular practice of silence has the effect of allowing you to temporarily withdraw and detach from the interactions of the world, thereby calming your mind over time. Silence allows you to discover the many things that do not need to be said. It awakens inner peace by allowing your inner voice a chance to respond to the multitude of thoughts and activities that you face dealing with the external world. When that inner voice starts to emerge, and you truly begin to listen, you will begin to recognize where illusion ends and truth begins. That inner voice does not speak through the mind, but through the heart—and the heart of truth will set you on a path to discover that true happiness cannot be found externally in the ever-changing material world of the ego-mind, but internally in the silence of a balanced mind, pure heart and peaceful spirit.

Exercise #1: The Pause of Silence

The next time you are engaged in a two-way conversation, whether on the phone or in person, pause for five seconds before responding to the other person. We are so accustomed to a constant state of chatter and noise that we often rush to reply without being fully conscious of what the other person said or how we responded. In our rush to say something, we lose the opportunity to listen, to truly listen, not only to the other person, but also to our own inner voice.

By pausing just five seconds before replying, you give yourself an opportunity to actively listen to the message that is being conveyed, understand the meaning of the message and reflect and listen to your Divine Inner Wisdom in order to respond in the most appropriate manner.

Exercise #2: Finding Peace in Silence

Try to set aside 30 waking minutes each day to be silent (either first thing in the morning or last thing before retiring) and witness the results. Try to pay attention to what you hear, see and feel—be the silent observer, the witness! This practice expands your awareness of your higher self—your innate intelligent spiritual self.

If you can expand this to one hour a day, I can assure you the transformation will be amazing!

Meditation is derived from two Latin words: *meditari* (to think, to dwell on, to exercise the mind), and *mederi* (to heal).

Some people may think of meditation as mental exercises or disciplines that enable them to achieve control over their mind, specifically to stop the vibrations of the ego-mind. Others may think of meditation as a way of life or a state of consciousness when their mind is free from scattered thoughts, patterns and habits.

The ego-mind is in constant movement, restless, distracted and reactive to emotions such as anger, desire, jealousy, hatred, fear or pain. The ego-mind is never at peace or content. Meditation, however, allows your mind to "rest" and attain a state of peace and harmony, which in turns allows your awareness to increase.

The theory of meditation is that when the mind and senses are controlled and transcended, the awareness of the transcendental state of consciousness becomes evident. As conscious awareness expands, the meditator taps latent abilities of the unconscious mind, and an immense feeling of joy emerges from within, and the desire for gratification from external sources fades. When you develop a transcendental mind, an inner confidence and knowing that you can meet the challenges of life arises, and you maintain a poised state of mind.

What form of meditation should you practice? Whatever form or technique works for you! You can meditate in silence or with sound, by yourself or in a group, indoors or outdoors. It's a matter of personal choice.

My own introduction to meditation came to me as a dare. Once upon a time I was a workaholic with an abundance of restless energy. Even on the weekends when I was not in the office I had to be doing something "productive": reading, writing, updating my three-page to-do list. One Sunday afternoon as I was puttering around the house, my husband said to me, "Come sit down on the couch for a few minutes." So I walked over to the loveseat and sat down, 15 seconds later, I got up (having scanned the room and noticing some papers that needed to be filed away). "What are you doing?" he asked. "I bet you can't sit down for five minutes" (the dare). "Okay, you are on!" I replied. This time I went into our bedroom, which had a window seat, and I sat there looking at the pine trees in the front yard. I must admit, I could stay still for only one minute at that point. Suddenly, an "aha" moment struck me and I decided to use a candle to help me stay put for more than a minute. Each day, I sat in our bedroom, placed a lit candle at eye level and watched the candle flame for two to three minutes. Once the image of the flame was firmly in my mind, I closed my eyes and gradually recreated the image of the flame in my third eye.

After one week, my candle meditation increased from 5 minutes to 10 minutes, and a few weeks later I was able to meditate for half an hour. My concentration and memory began to improve, and there were noticeable changes in my personality, as I no longer felt the need to control every minute of my day. Instead of updating my overbearing to-do list, I began to stop and smell the roses, enjoying my natural surroundings and spending more quality time with my family.

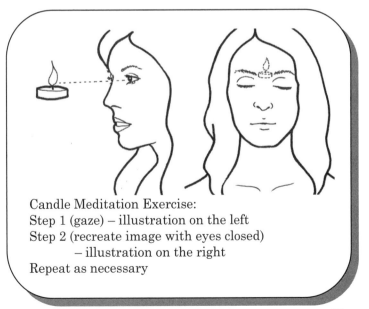

Candle Meditation Exercise:
Step 1 (gaze) – illustration on the left
Step 2 (recreate image with eyes closed)
        – illustration on the right
Repeat as necessary

With regular practice of silence and meditation, your ability to be introspective and examine your thoughts, habits and patterns of behavior will improve. And as you begin to observe yourself, you will realize what is truly important for your well-being, and find ways to balance your mind, body and spirit. As your awareness expands, you will naturally begin to release the patterns and behaviors that cause energy blocks, which in turn allows vital prana to flow through your body and personal vibration rates increase. Another benefit of meditation and silence is that they alter the brain waves from beta (agitation) to alpha, which is the level where healing begins to manifest.

Associate with Positive People

The company you keep also affects your personal vibration. If you mainly associate with people who are negative, angry and violent, then your interactions and experiences will be affected by the vibrations these people send out. Similarly, if you mainly associate with people who are positive, kind and benevolent, then your interactions and experiences will be affected by the vibrations of these people. There is one thing to remember, however, you can receive only vibrations to which you are attuned to receiving. In other words, if aspects of yourself—your beliefs, attitudes and expectations—are negative/low vibrations, then you are more open to receiving lower vibrations that others send out. Hence the importance of not only associating with positive people, but also of maintaining a positive outlook yourself!

According to the law of attraction, you are what you attract. Not only do birds of a feather flock together, so do people as well in terms of vibration dynamics. What we expect, believe and perceive, we receive back through our experiences, interactions and responses to situations. For example, angry people attract angry people and live in an angry world, and this validates their opinion that the world is angry.

Similarly, a chronic complainer or whiner expects problems and perceives that nothing is right with the world and, therefore, will attract experiences that are unpleasant, or find the unpleasantness in all situations in order to validate the need to complain. What is interesting is that complaining is a negative trait of low vibration and carries a low current of energy. Complainers usually seek out people with a higher vibration level and higher current of energy to "vent" to, because subconsciously they are in need of more energy.

Have you ever seen two complainers engaged in a conversation of any substantial length? Probably not, because neither one has sufficient energy to sustain the other. Instead, they will try to find someone with a higher vibration level in order to acquire more energy so they can continue to complain.

How to Handle Complainers

First, you can listen and show empathy, but you do not have to agree with them. Second, ask them what *they* plan to do about the situation? Without a plan of action, they will continue to dwell on negativity and keep on complaining.

Conserve your energy and limit the time you spend with complainers, especially if they are unwilling or refuse to take responsibility or action to resolve the issue.

How to Associate with Positive People

Step 1: Identify

Make a list of positive people you know from work, relatives, schoolmates and people from religious, recreational and other social organizations.

Step 2: Interact

Try to spend time with them. Whether it's a phone call, attending an event together or just hanging out, you will find positive people are confident and supportive and have an optimistic outlook on life. Their positive vibrations will be pleasantly infectious. When you surround yourself with people who have positive energy and are happy and well balanced, you too are more likely to be happy and well balanced.

Step 3: Reflect

Take time to reflect on the traits and characteristics that these positive people in your life possess. Reflect on how they respond to life's ups and downs. Learn from their experiences and wisdom to assist you in handling situations that arise in your own life.

When you make subtle changes in your own expectations/attitude to perceive the world in a more positive manner, you alter your vibrational frequency so that you become more attuned to receive positive and higher vibrations, and subsequently, you draw more positive and harmonious experiences into your life. This is the essence of the third vibrational law: *Changes in mental attitude and thoughts can affect the vibrational frequency of yourself, others you interact with and your experiences.*

Relationship Stress-Buster Rule:

The only person you can change is yourself!

Attitude of Gratitude

"Reflect upon your blessings, of which every man has plenty, not on your past misfortunes, of which all men have some."
~ Charles Dickens, 1812–1870

Developing an attitude of gratitude has tremendous effects on your emotional, mental and physical health. Have you ever noticed that some people can maintain a relatively positive attitude regardless of what's happening around them, even in the face of negative circumstances or events? They are able to see the good in difficult people, they see the opportunity in a challenging situation and they appreciate what they have, even in the face of loss. Would you like to increase your ability to maintain a positive attitude in your life, even in the face of challenging or stressful circumstances?

Fortunately, a positive attitude *can* be cultivated, with a little practice. Although we are born with specific temperamental tendencies, the brain is like a muscle that can be strengthened and trained toward optimism, if you work at it.

An attitude of gratitude can raise your vibration in seconds! When we focus on things we want or desire, we perceive the world from a place of "lack." We feel we do not have enough; we seek to obtain, to acquire by creating wants and desires. It is in the creation of wants and desires that the ego-mind flourishes and promotes dissatisfaction, restlessness and mental agitation. These negative feelings and thoughts use much energy, causing mental stress, which in turn suppresses our vibrational frequency.

However, when we feel blessed for what we do have, regardless of the present circumstance we are in, we perceive the world from a place of abundance, where our needs are being met. The mind is at ease when we maintain a positive attitude that we are adequately provided for. This mentality cultivates an attitude of gratitude.

Here are some exercises and tips to assist you in developing an attitude of gratitude:

Exercise #1
Each morning when you awake or each evening before bedtime, write down 10 things you are grateful for. Take time to reflect on each one and how it affects your life, well-being and sense of purpose. They can be profound or simple.

Exercise #2

Regard everyone you meet each day as a gift!
Remember to include the people you live with day
in and day out—those whom you sometimes take
for granted! When we are about to receive a gift,
we are often excited, curious and happy. You can
cultivate these qualities when you regard the
people who come in and out of your life each day.
Regard each interaction with someone as an opportunity to learn from them or an opportunity to
teach them or an opportunity to simply share an
experience together!

Exercise #3

If you find yourself making comparisons in ways
that make you feel inferior, then flip the mental
script and either (1) choose to compare yourself
with people who have less than you, which reminds you how truly fortunate you are, or (2) be
grateful for having people in your life who inspire
you, support you and love you. This will help lead
you away from stress and envy, and closer to feelings of gratitude.

Exercise #4

This is an exercise I do often with my own children. Say to your child, "I am lucky to have you in my life," and see the reaction. When my children were very young and I told them this, their faces became radiant! Then came the big smiles and lots of hugs. When they became teens and I told them, I usually got a raised eyebrow, then a smile, followed by hours of positive dialogue and discussion between us! When you tell others how terrific, awesome and brilliant they are, you not only raise your vibration by speaking positive words, but you send the recipient positive vibrations as well, which gives them an energy boost and raises their self-esteem and "feel-good" positive vibrations! Now you have two positively charged people interacting with each other in positive exchange! Try it and see what happens!

Try the above exercises for at least 21 consecutive days in order to cultivate a positive attitude of gratitude!

The Vibration
of Forgiveness

"To err is human, to forgive divine."
~ Alexander Pope, 1688–1744

It truly takes great effort to forgive someone who has hurt you, especially someone you have trusted and loved your entire life, someone who was your confidante, and your best friend. I am speaking from personal experience. I survived an attempted murder suicide that was initiated by my mother. How do you bring yourself to forgive someone of such a violent act?

The entire forgiveness process took me 16 years. I remember reliving the events of that day, but instead of thinking about what happened to me, I put myself in her world. I tried to think about what she was feeling and thinking that morning. What drove her to try to end my life and her own? And when I fully got into her consciousness, I came to the profound realization that this was a woman ravaged by fear—the fear of change and the fear of loss. These fears had plagued her since she was an infant and her mother died. When she was eight years old, her father died and she was raised by stepparents who neither treated her nor regarded her as their own child. She survived three miscarriages until, finally, I was born—her only child. And then some 20 years later, she was terrified of "losing" me and my love to my new husband and first child, who was on the way. She could not accept that I was a wife and a mother-to-be. All I can feel for her now is pity. After all, she had forgotten that love is infinite. I cannot love her less because I have two more people in my life to love. The more love I give, the more I have to give. I wholeheartedly forgave her and wished her the best life has to offer.

For me, forgiveness was about releasing the burden of the experience, and letting go of the negative emotions I felt in order to move forward with my life.

Forgiveness is truly about personal power. When you forgive someone, you take away their power and control over you. When you don't forgive, it is you who loses—because it is you who continues to hold onto the negative feelings, which eventually cause physical and emotional imbalance. Forgiveness does not necessarily mean reconciliation with the person who hurt you, or that you condone their actions. However, forgiveness is a process to finding peace.

Vibrational benefits of forgiveness:

- You lighten your heart by removing the heavy weight of the negative experiences(s).
- You lighten your speech when you stop complaining or accusing others of being responsible for your experiences.
- You lighten your emotions by releasing feelings of anger, frustration, spite and pain and make room for peace, joy and love.
- You are free! Forgiveness frees the forgiver. You are no longer enslaved to the circumstances you once thought were controlled by someone else or external forces. You are free to live and to love.
- Lastly, you gain strength by recognizing your ability to withstand any circumstance or experience—to learn from it—and move forward with your life.

Living in Joy

I give myself permission to enjoy all that I have now, and recognize and appreciate the good things in my life. I enjoy every moment.

What is Joy? Joy is ...

1. An emotion of great delight or happiness caused by something exceptionally good or satisfying; keen pleasure; elation.
2. A source or cause of keen pleasure or delight; something or someone greatly valued or appreciated.
3. The expression or display of glad feeling.
4. A state of happiness or felicity.

How can you experience more joy in your life? The first step is to realize that happiness and joy cannot come from objects that can be acquired, or from activities that can be performed. Happiness and joy can come only from within, because while one activity or object may seem pleasurable for one person, it may also be painful to another. This leads to the realization that it is not the activity or acquired object that holds the happiness, but the person who has assigned a value to it that she or he has been socialized to do. For the most part, the majority of people in North American society are socially conditioned to be dissatisfied with their present condition. As presented in "the vibration of media," we are continually told that we "do not have enough." If we allow these negative messages and images to embed in our psyche, then we will experience endless dissatisfaction, discontent and, eventually, depression.

Example of Discontent

Each week, millions of people buy lottery tickets with the thought that if they win, they will be happy or they will be free. They become full of dreams of a new life yet to be realized. But they do not pay attention to the negative psychological effects of dreaming of winning the lottery. First, in the hope of winning, they stir up their mind with countless visions of a new life, and this daydreaming and fantasizing agitates their mind. Second, if they do not win that week or that day, then the reaction is one of depression, thinking how they are stuck in their situation, and that nothing has improved in their life. Now, if the winning numbers were close to what they had selected, but still did not match, then they typically become angry and disappointed. This mental drama repeats itself week after week, as they ride the roller coaster of hopefulness, then despair, with each ticket purchased. As they continually depend on external factors to find a sense of happiness and joy, their busy ego-mind will not allow for feelings of peace or contentment. Similar habits are observed in people who continually need to buy new clothes or new furnishngs/renovate in order to feel better. Remember the adage, even if you try to "get away from it all," "wherever you go, there you are!" You cannot run away from yourself, nor lose yourself in new clothes, new furnishings or hopes of winning the lottery!

The feelings of dissatisfaction and desire generated by your ego-mind will continually overpower your higher mind/reasoning mind until you are committed to replacing your value system with one that allows you to appreciate all that you have *now*—in this *present* moment! If you continue to dwell on what was, you will create an environment of resentment, and if you continue to fantasize on what might be/might happen, you create an environment of stress and dissatisfaction.

If you value joy, then be joyful for what you have—such as family who love you, the ability to laugh, to breathe! Be joyful for what you are able to give—such as volunteering your time for those less fortunate than you, a warm smile to a stranger and seeing them smile back, sharing your knowledge and skills with others for their growth and development, a hug! I remember volunteering a few hours a month at my children's daycare and observing the children interact with each other. Young children are naturally curious, kind and compassionate and seem to make friends at the drop of a hat. As we grow older, these natural tendencies seem to fade as we are conditioned by society's countless rules and expectations from parents, teachers, church, employers and others. If we can resurrect the curiosity of our youth, then perhaps we can once again enjoy the many simple pleasures life offers us every moment of every day.

I share with you some famous quotations on joy and happiness—as a reminder of why we are all here now.

Famous Quotations:
"The moment one gives close attention to any thing, even a blade of grass, it becomes a mysterious, awesome, indescribably magnificent world in itself."
~ Henry Miller, 1891–1980

"If my heart can become pure and simple like that of a child, I think there probably can be no greater happiness than this."
~ Kitaro Nishida, 1870–1945

"Slow down and enjoy life. It's not only the scenery you miss by going too fast—you also miss the sense of where you are going and why."
~ Eddie Cantor, 1892–1964

"There are those who give with joy, and that joy is their reward."
~ Kahlil Gibran, 1883–1931

"The foolish man seeks happiness in the distance; the wise man grows it under his feet."
~ James Oppenheim, 1882–1932

"Happiness is like a butterfly, which, when you pursue it is always beyond your grasp, but, which, when you sit down may alight upon you."
~ Nathaniel Hawthorne, 1804–1864

"Peace comes from within. Do not seek it without."
~ Buddha, c. 563–483 BCE

"Find ecstasy in life; the mere sense of living is joy enough."
~ Emily Dickinson, 1830–1886

"The greater part of happiness or misery depends on our dispositions, not our circumstances."
~ Martha Washington, 1731–1802

Your ability to experience inner peace and contentment and joy is strengthened by your willpower to change your values and learn to recognize and appreciate the good things life offers. It is also strengthened by your discipline to apply the exercises and knowledge you have attained in this book, and your commitment to enjoy the moment!

A Summary of What You Have Learned

By applying the exercises presented in the previous chapters, you will have learned a few new things about yourself.

- You will have learned the interconnectedness of thoughts, emotions and actions and how positive thoughts and a positive outlook resonate through every aspect of your life.

- You will be able to increase the vital life force energy through breath work and reconnecting with nature.

- You will recognize the importance of consuming high-vibrational foods and drink (i.e., organic, natural, raw and nutrient rich) to adequately nourish your body, maintain cellular health, increase vitality and repel disease.

- You will understand the vital link between detoxification and raising the internal vibrations of your organs, fluids and cells so they operate as they were intended—without stress and imbalance.

- Your interactions with others will have become more harmonious, as you have learned to actively listen, and consciously respond in a more meaningful and peaceful manner.

- By practicing silence, meditation and an attitude of gratitude, the need to judge, control or change others will dissipate, while your acceptance, appreciation and understanding of others expands.

- You will have discovered the healing properties of gems and crystals, sound and color and be able to draw out negative and low vibrations and bring in positive and higher vibrations into your aura and chakras.

- You will be more discerning about your consumption of mass media and the company that you keep, recognizing that they can drain your positive energy and lower your personal vibration very quickly.

- You will know that you are the creator of vibrations and you can attune yourself to receive beneficial and higher vibrations based on your thoughts, beliefs, attitude and expectations.

- As you quiet your ego-mind, you will hear your inner voice of Divine Wisdom, and as you listen, your confidence and trust will grow with the knowing that you can meet all the challenges that life presents, and know that you are able to choose the best response to all circumstances your encounter. It is in this inner knowing that life can truly be enjoyed.

Living in Love

My Daily Affirmation: *Praise Love above me, praise Love below me, praise Love around me, praise Love within me, Love is all I am, Love is all I have, Love is all I need. Love is all I give.*

Repeat this affirmation seven times to anchor the vibration of love within your core being. It reminds me that I have all that I need and all that I need is within me. I cannot think of a better way to start my day—remembering that I am love—the highest vibration there is!

All paths of raising one's personal vibration ultimately lead to love. The more love you send out, the more love comes back to you.

The Path of Love and Vibration

By actively choosing to raise your personal vibration, you are choosing to love yourself by removing stress and regaining vitality, by transcending your ego-mind to your higher mind of Divine Wisdom and by living in harmony to experience oneness with all aspects of yourself. Self-love is like the seed from which love for all others is born.

It is difficult to love others if you do not love yourself. Furthermore, the relationship you have with yourself mirrors the relationship you have with others. If you do not have love for some aspect of yourself, then you draw to you those who vibrate in resonance with that aspect of your energy. The more you continue to look at what you don't like, don't have or don't want, the more you draw those things to you. Conversely, the more you see love, hear love, feel love in all you experience in life, then the more loving your world becomes.

At times you may experience pain, suffering or stress, but now you are equipped with the knowledge that all circumstances can be transformed by raising your vibration, awareness and perception.

You posses the creative, intelligent, infinite power to transform any condition and transcend any situation by resonating the vibration of love!

You are capable of manifesting the best of yourself when you are committed to taking positive action to raising your vibration. Take action to resonate love and experience love, because life is love—the highest vibration in the universe!

I leave you with a quote from the Scottish mountaineer and writer W. H. Murray, paraphrasing Goethe, on the importance of commitment.[23]

Until one is committed, there is hesitancy, the chance to draw back, always ineffectiveness. Concerning all acts of initiative (and creation), there is one elementary truth the ignorance of which kills countless ideas and splendid plans: that the moment one definitely commits oneself, then providence moves too. All sorts of things occur to help one that would never otherwise have occurred. A whole stream of events issues from the decision, raising in one's favor all manner of unforeseen incidents, meetings and material assistance, which no man could have dreamed would have come his way.

And lastly, remember this:

All you need is within you!

Your Notes

Use this section to make notes on important concepts and facts you have learned.

_____

_____

_____

_____

_____

_____

_____

_____

_____

_____

_____

_____

_____

_____

_____

_____

_____

_____

Personal Action Plan

Use this section to select and record the exercises you will incorporate into your daily schedule. As you progress week by week, try to increase the duration of certain exercises (i.e., meditation, breathing techniques, activities you enjoy doing).

High-Vibration Actions	Week 1	Week 2	Week 3	Week 4
	Duration (minutes)	Duration (minutes)	Duration (minutes)	Duration (minutes)
Morning exercise(s):				
Afternoon exercise(s):				
Evening exercise(s):				
What brings me joy:				
Positive people I know and will spend time with:				
I demonstrate a love for life by:				

Glossary

Alternative medicine: The practice of medicine without the use of drugs; may involve herbal medicines, chiropractic, shiatsu, biofeedback, acupuncture, faith healing, energy healing.

Aura: An energy field that is held to emanate from a living being.

Authentic power: The harmonious alignment of the personality with the soul.

Bikram yoga: A style of yoga developed by Bikram Choudhury. Ideally, it is practiced in a room heated to 103°F. Choudhury claims that blood circulation is affected immensely during Bikram yoga because of two processes called *extension* and *compression*. These two dynamics are said to work together to deliver fresh oxygen to every joint, muscle and organ within the human body.

Biochemical: Characterized by, produced by, or involving chemical reactions in living organisms.

Bioelectric: Bioelectricity refers to electrical potentials and currents occurring within or produced by living organisms.

Brainwave entrainment: Using binaural frequencies to entrain the brain so that the left and right hemispheres work together in a state of coherence.

Cell mutation: Adverse changes in the DNA sequence of a cell's genome that may be caused by radiation, viruses or mutagenic chemicals (i.e., typically carcinogens), as well as errors that may occur during chromosome division or DNA replication.

Chakra: Any of several points of physical or spiritual energy in the human body, according to yoga philosophy; also referred to as the wheel of light.

Chromotherapy: Based on the premise that certain colors are infused with healing energies. The therapy uses the seven colors of the rainbow to promote balance and healing in the mind and body.

Denatured: To deprive of natural qualities, change the nature of; to modify the molecular structure of (as a protein or DNA), especially by heat, acid, alkali or ultraviolet radiation so as to destroy or diminish some of the original properties, and especially the specific biological activity.

DNA: Deoxyribonucleic acid: A nucleic acid, usually of very high molecular weight, consisting of a linear sequence of monomer units of deoxyribonucleotides, occurring in most organisms in pairs of strands, wound together in the form of a double helix; it is the main component of chromosomes and contains the genetic information that is the basis of heredity, transmitted from parent to progeny, and found in all living organisms except for certain viruses that have RNA (ribonucleic acid) as their basic genetic material.

Electromagnetic: Pertaining to or exhibiting magnetism produced by an electric charge in motion.

Hemispheric synchronization: See brainwave entrainment.

Hertz (Hz): A unit of frequency equal to one cycle per second.

Infrared sauna: An infrared sauna uses infrared heaters to emit infrared radiant heat that is absorbed directly into the human body, unlike traditional saunas that heat the body indirectly via air or steam.

Ma'at: From Egyptian mythology, the goddess of the physical and moral law of Egypt, of order and truth. Typically depicted in the form of a woman holding a scepter in one hand and an ankh in the other.

Mantra: A prayer, an invocation, a religious formula, a charm.

Meridian: Any of the pathways along which the body's vital energy flows according to the theory behind acupuncture.

Monochord: A droning harmonic sound-generating chamber that resembles a giant harp or guitar. This instrument involves tuning 28 bronze strings to the same note.

Nadi: Channels through which subtle energy moves.

Prana: Vital energy of the universe present within every living thing, also known as Qi, Ki, chi, universal life force energy.

Prime resonant frequency: The optimal vibrational frequency of an organ, tissue or cell.

Sentient: Endowed with feeling and unstructured consciousness; to discern or perceive by the senses.

Sonic signature: A sound wave with characteristics specific to an area or region.

Sonocytology: The study of the sound of cells.

Tambura (South India); Tanpura (North India): A drone instrument that as no frets. It has four strings that are tuned to the tonic; it provides a firm harmonic base for the music.

Universal life force energy: Vital energy of the universe present within every living thing, also known as Qi, Ki, chi, prana.

Vibrational frequency: The constant rate of electrical flow that is measurable between two points.

Vishnu Mudra: A hand gesture used to alternate the breath through the nostrils, whereby index and middle finger are bent into the center of one's palm while doing the breath work exercise.

References

1. Masuru Emoto, *The Miracle of Water* (New York: Atria books, 2007).
2. André Dollinger, comp., "Ancient Egyptian Texts: The 'Negative Confessions' from the Papyrus of Ani, c. 1240 BCE. The Declaration of Innocence from the Book of the Dead," trans. E. A. Wallis Budge, www.reshafim.org.il/ad/egypt/negative_confessions/ index.html (accessed January 2, 2010).
3. Thinking Allowed Productions, "Conversations on the Leading Edge of Knowledge and Discovery with Jeffrey Mishlove: *The Seat of the Soul* with Gary Zukav," 1998, www.williamjames.com/transcripts/zukav.htm (accessed January 2, 2010).
4. The Center for Food Safety. "A Message from Anna Lappé: Help Us Fight for a New Food Future!" http://truefoodnow.org/campaigns/a-message-from-anna-lappe (accessed January 11, 2010).
5. Helke Ferrie, "Food Fight," *Vitality Magazine*, July/August 2009, 10.
6. Mary Ruth Swope, *Green Leaves of Barley: Inspiring Secrets of Nature's Miracle Rejuvenator* (Phoenix, AZ: Swope Enterprises, 1987), 33.
7. Keiichi Morishita, *Hidden Truth of Cancer*, trans. Herman Aihara (Chico, CA: George Ohsawa Macrobiotic Foundation, 1976).

8. Nuconcepts Inc., "Dr. Otto Warburg," 2000,
http://nuconceptsinc.com/Dr.%20Otto%20Warburg.htm
(accessed January 3, 2010).

9. A. G. Schauss, Keynote Lecture (Texas Conference on Nutrition and Behavior, University of Texas at Austin, October 28, 1982); and A. G. Schauss, "Nutrition and Behavior," *Journal of Applied Nutrition* 35 (1983):30–43.

10. Organic Trade Association, "Soil Health," July 2002,
www.ota.com/organic/environment/soil.html
(accessed January 4, 2010).

11. Sally Fallon and Mary G. Enig, "Be Kind to Your Grains and Your Grains Will Be Kind to You," The Weston A. Price Foundation, 1999, www.westonaprice.org/be-kind-to-your-grains...and-your-grains-will-be-kind-to-you.html
(accessed January 4, 2010).

12. Digestives Plus, "Enzymes,"
www.digestivesplus.com/enzymes.html
(accessed January 5, 2010).

13. AvianWeb, "The 'Downside' of Coffee,"
http://www.avianweb.com/coffeeandcaffeine.html#neg
(accessed January 12, 2010).

14. Marie Wolfe, "World's Top Sweetener Is Made with GM Bacteria," *The Independent*, June 20, 1999,
www.independent.co.uk/news/worlds-top-sweetener-is-made-with-gm-bacteria-1101176.html (accessed January 5, 2010).

15. Sae Bae Lee et al., "United States Patent US5030567: Method for Production of L-Phenylalanine by Recombinant *E. coli* ATCC 67460," July 9, 1991,
www.freepatentsonline.com/5030567.pdf
(accessed January 5, 2010).

16. Minnesota Wellness Productions, Inc., "Cleaning House: The Correct Way to Detox," 2009, www.mnwelldir.org/docs/detox/clean.htm (accessed January 5, 2010).

17. Earthtym, "Acid-Alkaline pH Chemical Balance," www.earthtym.net/ph-intro.htm (accessed January 6, 2010).

18. Biocybernaut Institute, "Alpha Brain Waves," 2005, www.biocybernaut.com/about/brainwaves/alpha.htm (accessed January 6, 2010).

19. Yogi Ramacharaka, "The Hundu-Yogi Science of Breath," p. 16, www.hermetics.org/pdf/ScienceOfBreath.pdf (accessed January 6, 2010).

20. Essential-Oils-for-Health.com, "Discovering How Essential Oils Are Different from Herbs and Food Supplements Is an Important Step in Learning the Variety of Ways to Use These Powerful Plant Oils," www.essential-oils-for-health.com/therapeutic-essential-oils.html (accessed January 6, 2010).

21. Essential Science Publishing, comp., *Essential Oils Desk Reference*, 2nd ed., (Hurricane, UT: Essential Science Publishing, 2001).

22. Laura De Giorgio, "Deep Trance Now: Color Therapy— Chromotherapy," www.deeptrancenow.com/colortherapy.htm (accessed January 6, 2010).

23. W. H. Murray, *The Scottish Himalayan Expedition* (London: J. M. Dent & Sons, 1951).

About the Author

Dawn James is a vibrational healer, teacher, speaker and writer. Her parents discovered she was an empathic intuit at age three, and at the same time she fell in love with music and sound and began studies in piano and music theory at the Royal Conservatory of Music in Toronto, Canada. Later, as a teenager, she began having precognitive dreams that continued into adulthood. Her spiritual journey has brought her insights and extensive knowledge of holistic and esoteric matters and vibrational frequency. Following a near-death experience in 2003, Dawn received several spiritual gifts, including the gift of healing. Although she is formally trained in Reiki and distance healing, she specializes in vibrational healing because she believes that it is a pure, intelligent and effective method for healing mind, body and spirit. She is the mother of three young adults, and resides in Ontario, Canada with her husband. Dawn conducts workshops and speaks throughout Canada and the United States on matters relating to holistic health, stress-less living, vibrational frequency and healing with sound. For more information, please visit www.raiseyourvibration.ca.

ORDER FORM

 PO Box 1665
Brighton, ON
K0K 1H0

BULK DISCOUNTS AVAILABLE.
Please call us toll-free at 1-888-767-8423

Please fill out this form and mail with your check or money order to Lotus Moon Press at the address above.

Please rush me_____copies of *Raise Your Vibration, Transform Your Life* @ $21.95 Cdn or USD	$
Postage & Handling $3.00/copy Cdn/US	$
Subtotal	$
5% GST tax for Canadian orders (subtotal x 0.05) BN#133760579	$
TOTAL – please check either ◯Cdn$ ◯US$	$
Ship to Name:	
Organization:	
Address:	
City:	State/Prov
Country:	Zip/P.C.
Phone:	Fax:
Email:	

Note: Order **10 or more books** and receive a significant discount plus **FREE** shipping & handling. Please contact the publisher at **1-888-767-8423** for bulk discount pricing.